FIRST 50
BLUEGRASS SONGS
YOU SHOULD PLAY ON BANJO

by Fred Sokolow

Editorial assistance by Ronny S. Schiff

ISBN 1-96288-09809-6

Visit Hal Leonard Online at
www.halleonard.com

World headquarters, contact:
Hal Leonard
7777 West Bluemound Road
Milwaukee, WI 53213
Email: info@halleonard.com

In Europe, contact:
Hal Leonard Europe Limited
1 Red Place
London, W1K 6PL
Email: info@halleonardeurope.com

In Australia, contact:
Hal Leonard Australia Pty. Ltd.
4 Lentara Court
Cheltenham, Victoria, 3192 Australia
Email: info@halleonard.com.au

INTRODUCTION

You're looking at a collection of essential songs for the bluegrass banjo player— songs that are performed and recorded by countless bluegrass bands, and songs you will be expected to know at bluegrass jam sessions. Some of the songs are transcribed exactly as they were played by a pioneering banjo player like Earl Scruggs or Ralph Stanley. Others are the author's arrangements; they stay close to the song's melody and are mostly "Scruggs style," with an occasional melodic ("Keith style") lick.

In some songs, the verse and chorus are musically identical, though the lyrics differ. In songs of this type, two solos are often presented, one in first position and one up the neck, so you can see a variety of ways to approach a solo. Other songs' choruses are completely different from their verses. In these cases, you'll find solos written out for the verse, as that's what the soloist usually plays.

Special bonus: When a solo in this collection is transcribed from a recording by a well-known picker, there are notes that tell you on which album it can be found, so you can hear it on YouTube and, in most cases, slow it down. When a solo is the author's arrangement, it's helpful to listen to the song on YouTube, or whichever platform you use to listen to music. You won't hear the exact written arrangement...even so, listening (before working on the solo) is highly recommended! Having the tune in your head makes it much easier to learn a piece from tab/music.

Most of the songs in this collection were made popular by bands from the "golden age" of bluegrass—the 1950s: Bill Monroe and His Bluegrass Boys, Flatt and Scruggs and the Foggy Mountain Boys, the Stanley Brothers and the Clinch Mountain Boys, Reno and Smiley and the Tennessee Cutups, Jim and Jesse McReynolds and the Virginia Boys, and so on. The tunes have stood the test of time and are still heard at bluegrass festivals and concerts all over the world. Learn how to solo over them and you're building the repertoire you need, to play bluegrass with other pickers. Hopefully, in the process of learning these arrangements you'll also learn the licks, styles and techniques that will enable you to make up your own bluegrass-style banjo solos.

Good luck and good picking!

Fred Sokolow

Fred Sokolow

SOME PRELIMINARY NOTES

• The lyrics written above the tab are there to help you correlate the solos to the songs. You don't normally sing while playing solos. Additional lyrics are also presented, so you can perform these songs in their entirety, in addition to playing solos.

• About capos and re-tuning the 5th string: Bluegrass banjo players favor the key of G, since the banjo is almost always tuned to an open G chord (GDGBD), and so many iconic bluegrass banjo licks are played in G tuning. But pickers must know how to play in any key. The capo makes it possible to play G licks in the keys of A, B♭, B, or C: put the capo on the 2nd fret for A, 3rd fret for B♭, 4th fret for B and 5th fret for C...and tune the 5th string up to the key note (e.g., tune the 5th string to a B note to play in the key of B), or use a 5th string capo or have spikes installed.

• Fiddle tunes are almost always played in a certain key. For example, "Soldier's Joy" is always played in the key of D. The arrangement in this book is written in the key of C, with instructions to capo up two frets and tune the 5th string to A. This puts you in the key of D (it's two frets higher than C). That's the way most banjo players would play it. But the tune is written in respect to the capo, as if it's in C.

• Most fiddle tunes have two sections: an A and B part. Typically, to go once around the tune, you play AABB.

• Bluegrass pickers sometimes play in the keys of C, D, E or F without using a capo...they just re-tune the 5th string. You'll find some examples in this book.

• When a chord letter name is in parentheses (C), it means the song has that chord change, but the banjo is not playing the chord shape.

Can't You Hear Me Callin'

Words and Music by Bill Monroe

This bluesy, tortured love song is one of many Bill Monroe tunes inspired by Bessie Lee Mauldin, who toured, sang and played bass with the Bluegrass Boys for many years. The following banjo solo is from an exceptional live Bill Monroe performance that features the singing of Mac Wiseman, a brilliant bluegrass tenor, and the banjo playing of Don Reno. (The verses have the same melody and chords as the chorus.)

G tuning:
(5th-1st) G-D-G-B-D

Key of G

Verse

Moderately

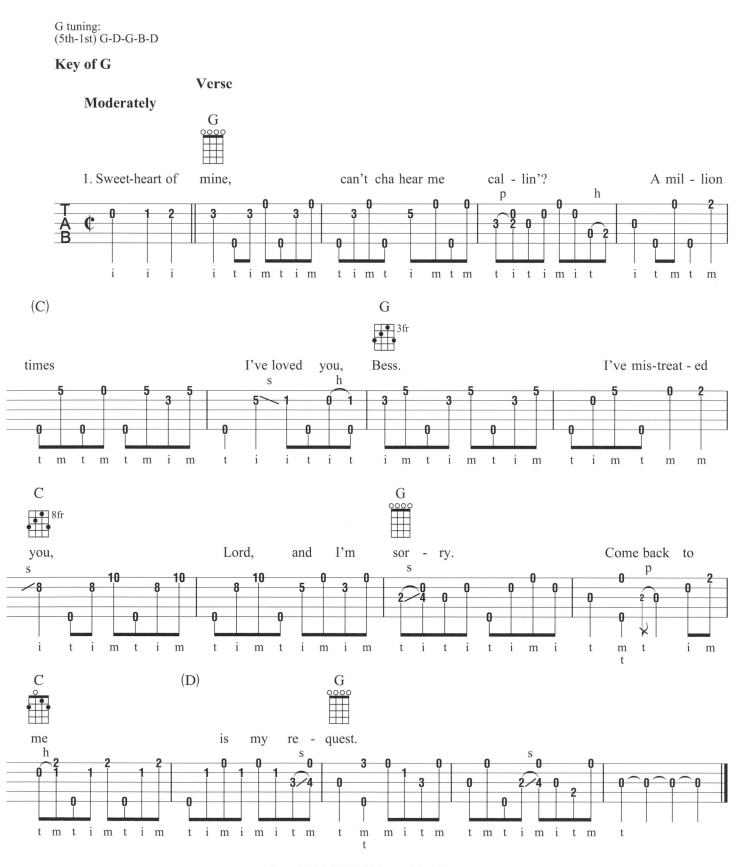

Ballad of Jed Clampett

from the Television Series THE BEVERLY HILLBILLIES
Words and Music by Paul Henning

Written as a theme song for the television series "The Beverly Hillbillies" (1962–1971), "Ballad of Jed Clampett" tells the story on which the show was based. On the TV show, country singer Jerry Scoggins sang the "Ballad…" at a leisurely country tempo, accompanied by Flatt and Scruggs, who then kicked it up to a fast bluegrass, cut-time instrumental. With the success of the show, Flatt and Scruggs released a more traditional bluegrass version of the song, with Flatt singing it. It was the first bluegrass song to spend five months on the pop charts.

Scruggs' solo is written, below. He's capoed up two frets, with his fifth string tuned up to A, to play in the key of A.

G tuning:
(5th-1st) G-D-G-B-D

Key of G

Moderately fast

Verse

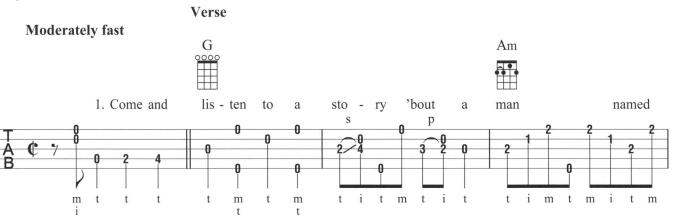

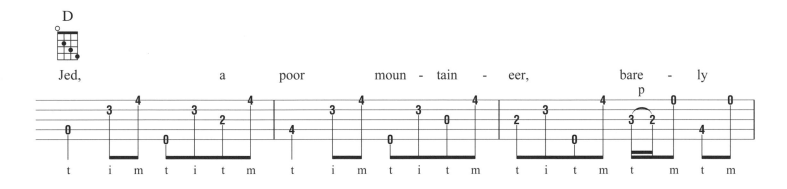

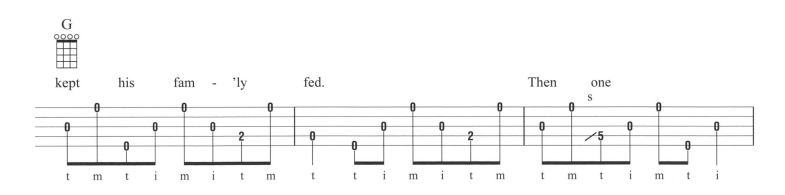

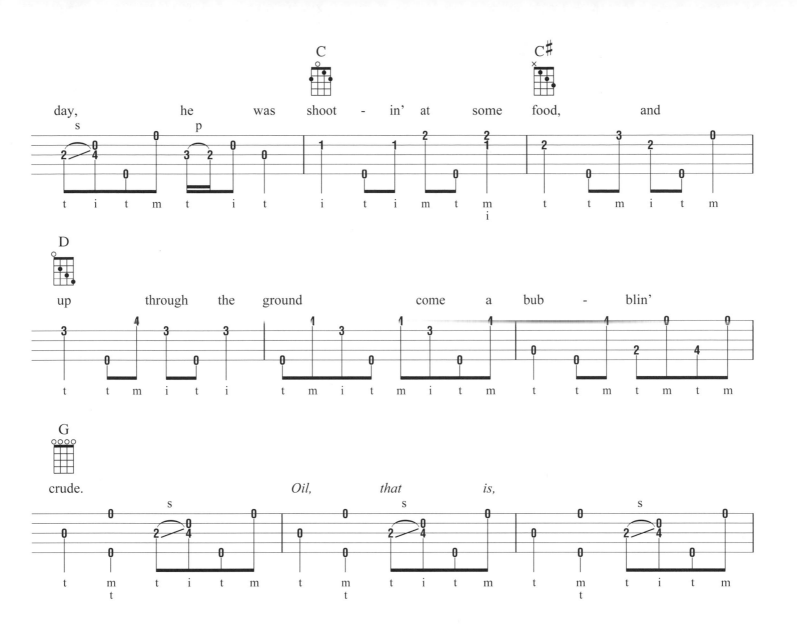

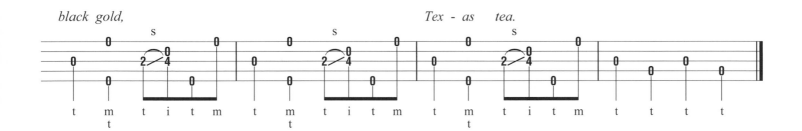

Additional Lyrics

2. First thing you know, old Jed's a millionaire.
Kin folks said, "Jed, move away from there."
Said, California was the place he ought to be,
So they loaded up the truck and they moved to Beverly.
Hills, that is, swimming pools, movie stars.

3. Well, now it's time to say goodbye to Jed and all his kin.
They would like to thank you folks for kindly dropping in.
You're all invited back next week to this locality,
To have a heaping helping of their hospitality.
Beverly Hillbillies, that's what they call 'em now.
Nice folks. Y'all come back now, hear?

Bill Cheatham

Traditional

"Bill Cheatham," a key-of-A fiddle tune, has been played by countless string bands and bluegrass groups, ever since the late 1800s. It has the AABB format typical of fiddle tunes: An eight-bar phrase (A) is repeated (A again), then there's a different phrase (B) that is also repeated (B again). When you play AABB, you've gone once around the tune. The following arrangement goes twice around the tune, first in a low register, then up the neck.

This arrangement is in G, but if you capo up two frets and tune the fifth string up to A, you'll be in the key of A. Some of the chord grids are not actually chords, they are fingering positions that allow you to play scalar, melodic licks. The "Intro" bar that is repeated four time initiates many fiddle tunes; it's sometimes referred to as "potatoes," as in "Give me four potatoes to kick off this tune."

G tuning:
(5th-1st) G-D-G-B-D

Key of G

Intro

Fast

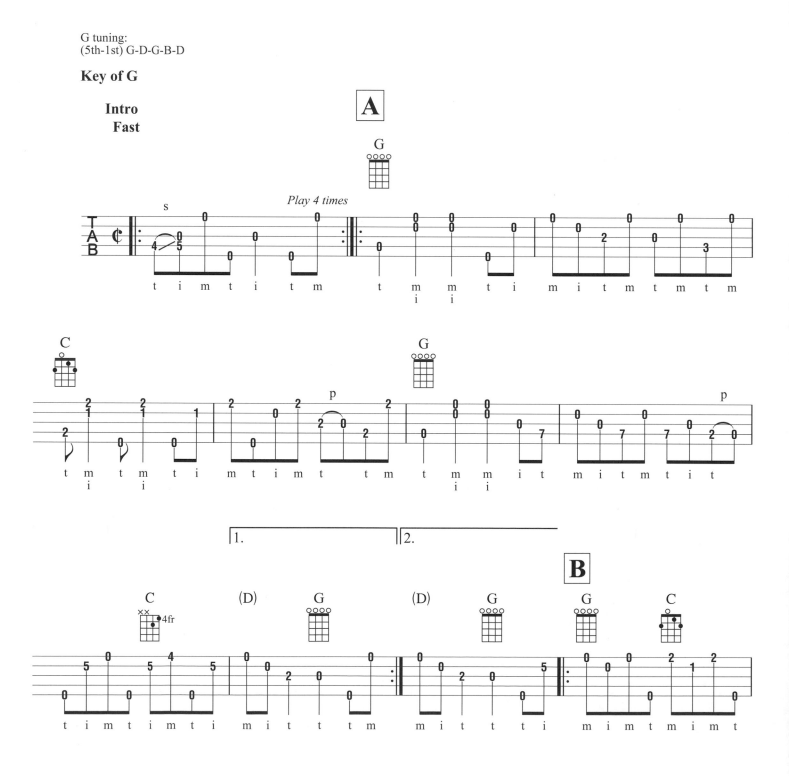

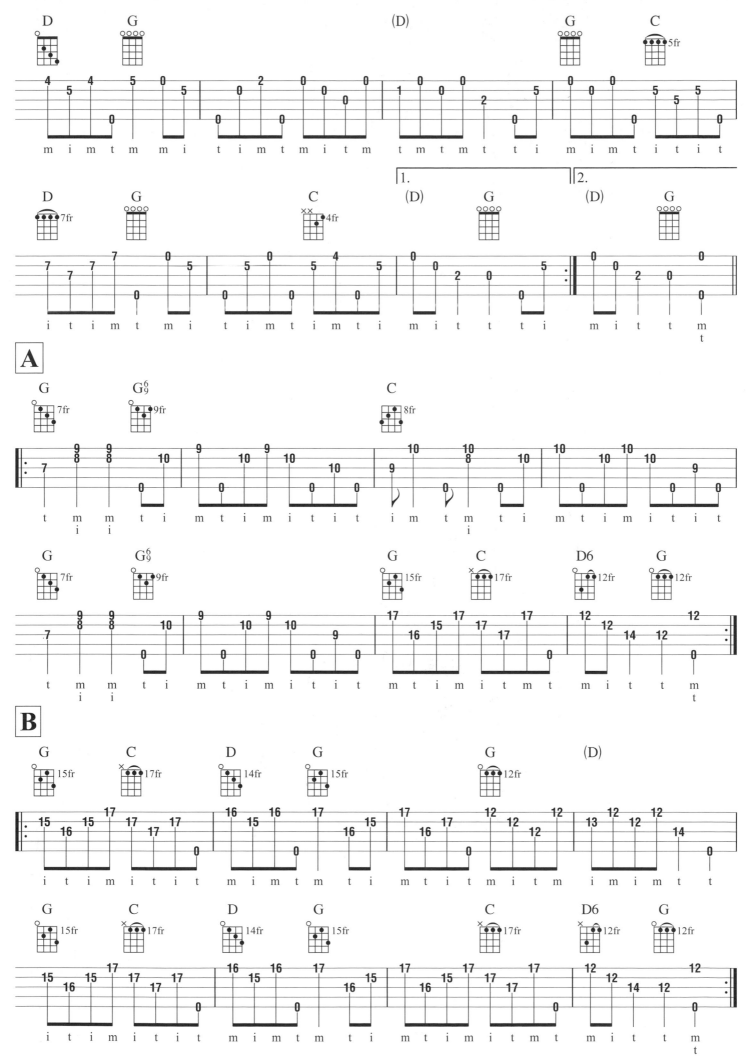

Blackberry Blossom

Traditional

It may have come from Ireland, but American fiddler Arthur Smith brought this fiddle tune to the attention of country and old-time music fans in the 1930s. Then, in the early 1960s, Bill Keith's banjo version made it a bluegrass standard—the pretty melody is a good showcase for Keith's innovative "melodic picking" style. It has become an essential bluegrass instrumental.

Like most fiddle tunes in the bluegrass repertoire, it is nearly always played in a certain key—in this case, the key of G. Notice that "Blackberry Blossom" has the typical AABB format. This arrangement presents two versions of the tune: one in Scruggs style, the other in melodic style, which allows you to more closely duplicate scalar fiddle licks. Notice that you need to fret the fifth string, to play the B7 in the first B part; it can be fretted with your index finger, but some pickers find it easier to reach over the neck with their thumb and fret it that way.

G tuning:
(5th-1st) G-D-G-B-D

Key of G

Fast

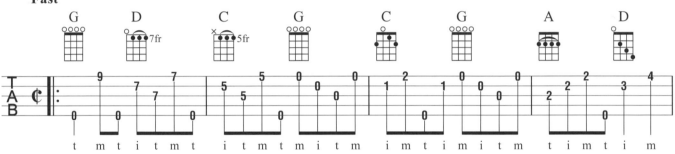

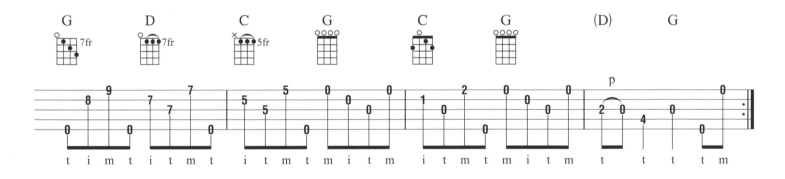

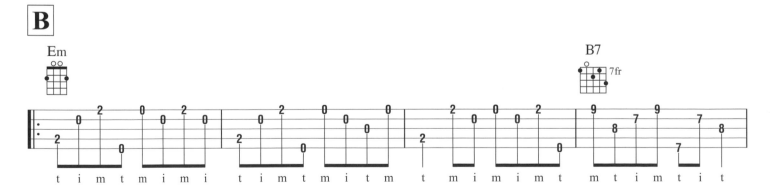

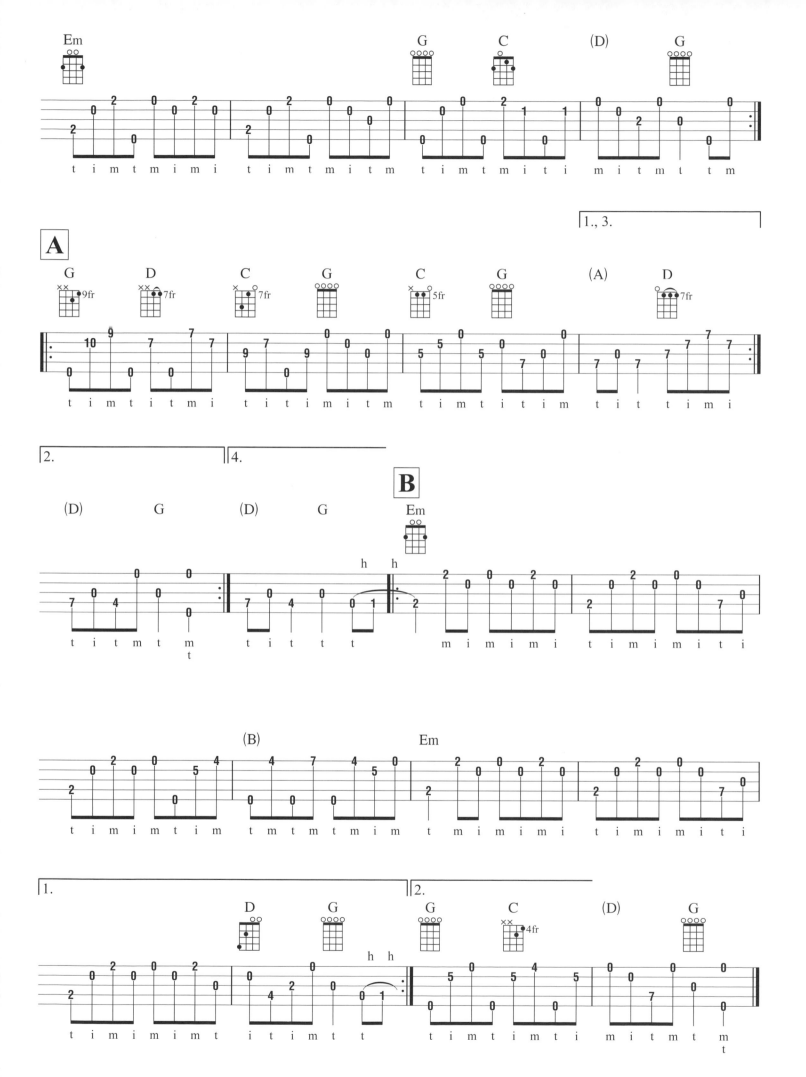

Blue Moon of Kentucky

Words and Music by Bill Monroe

Bill Monroe had already scored a hit with his "Kentucky Waltz" when he wrote "Blue Moon of Kentucky," and it eventually became his signature song and Kentucky's state song. In 1954, Elvis Presley recorded it but changed the tempo from a waltz to an upbeat rockabilly romp…so Monroe re-recorded it, starting it as a waltz, then kicking it into a fast, cut-time, bluegrass beat…and that's how most bluegrassers play it today.

G tuning:
(5th-1st) G-D-G-B-D

Key of C

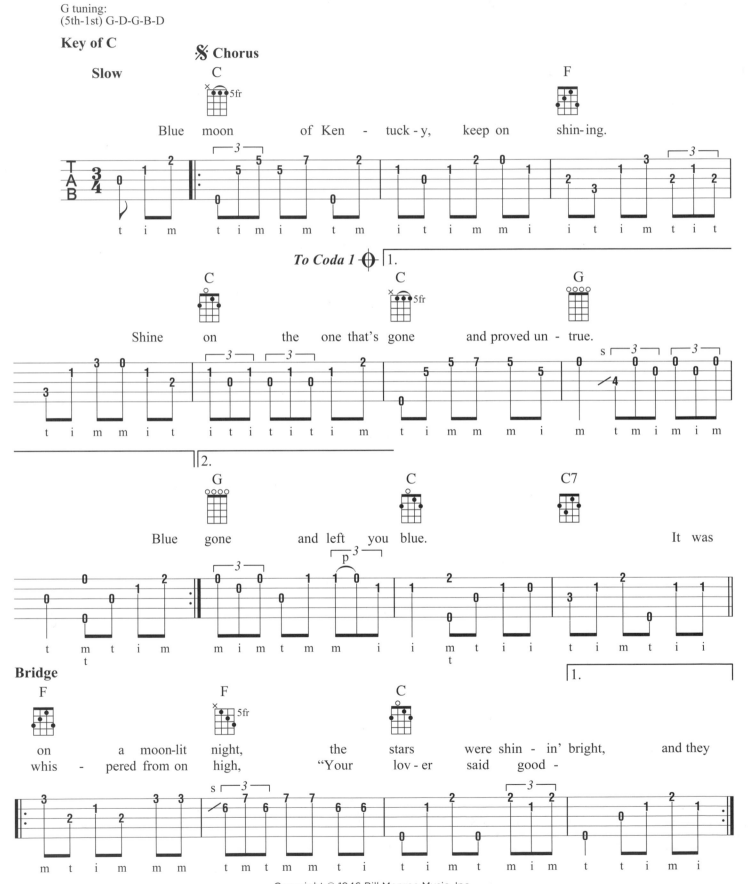

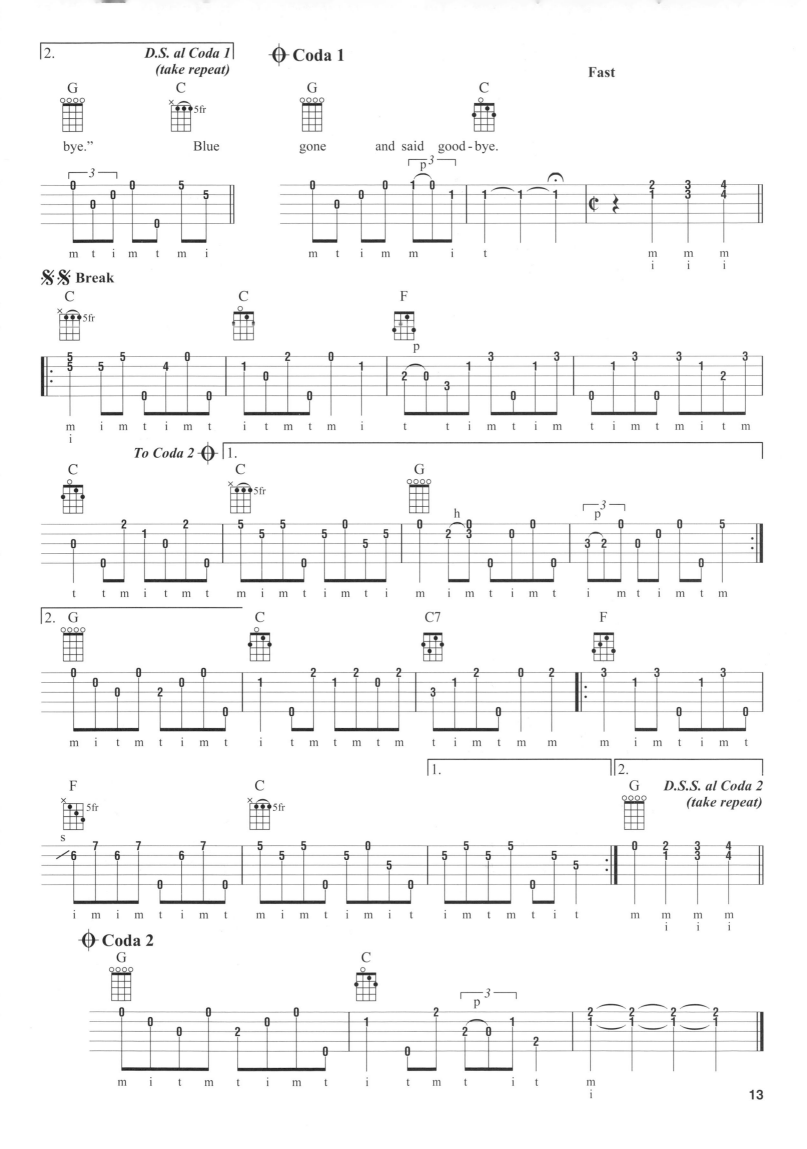

Bury Me Beneath the Willow

Traditional

The Carter Family recorded this old folk song in 1927 at the famous Bristol Sessions where they and Jimmie Rodgers were discovered. However, the tune was archived by a music professor in 1906, and it probably is much older than that. The verse and chorus share the same melody. In this arrangement, the verse is played in first position, the chorus is up the neck. The final "G" chord at the end of the tune is really an Em, but it's a moveable chord position that is often used to play G licks.

G tuning:
(5th-1st) G-D-G-B-D

Key of G

Moderately

Verse

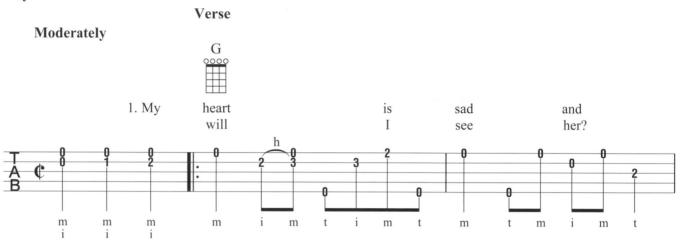

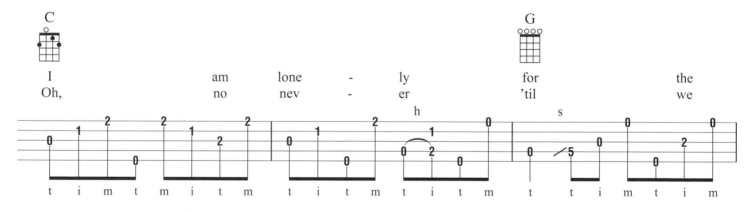

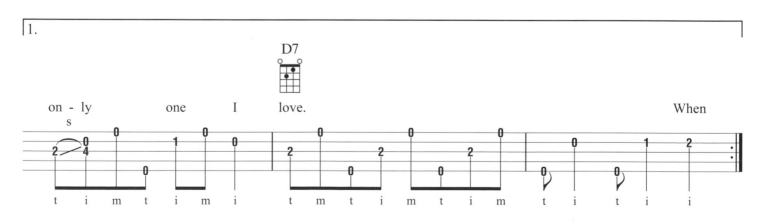

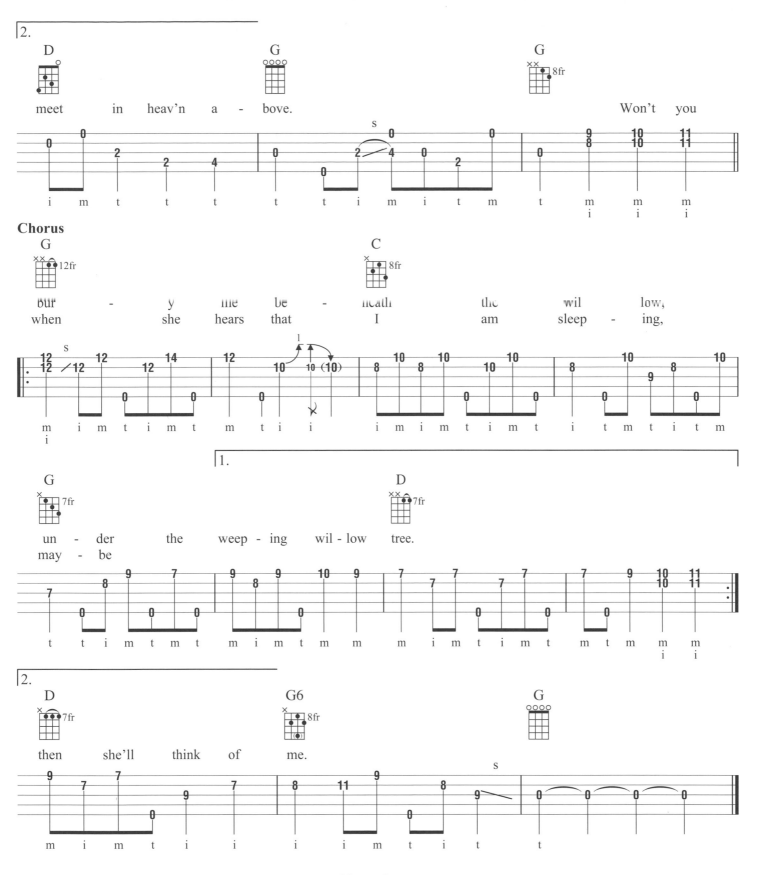

Additional Lyrics

2. They told me that she did not love me,
   I could not believe it's true,
   Until an angel softly whispered,
   "She no longer cares for you."

3. Tomorrow was to be our wedding.
   Lord, oh Lord, where can she be?
   She's gone, she's gone to find another.
   She no longer cares for me.

Cash on the Barrelhead

Words and Music by Charles Louvin and Ira Louvin

This colorful story song was written and recorded by the Louvin Brothers, a popular country duo who scored many hits in the late 1950s and early '60s. Several of their songs have become bluegrass and country standards. "Cash on the Barrelhead" has been recorded by Jim and Jesse McReynolds, Rhonda Vincent, Alison Krauss, Bill Monroe and Dolly Parton (on her *The Grass Is Blue* album)…to mention a few. The song's title is an old expression meaning "immediate payment," because some honky tonk bars had barrels for tables, and customers were obliged to pay for their drinks by putting cash on the barrel tops.

If you listen to any bluegrass version of "Cash on the Barrelhead," you'll hear frequent "stops," moments when the band stops playing for a beat. The banjo makes those stops happen with rhythmic "pinches," in which the 1st and 5th strings are picked, simultaneously.

G tuning:
(5th-1st) G-D-G-B-D

Key of G

Moderately

Verse

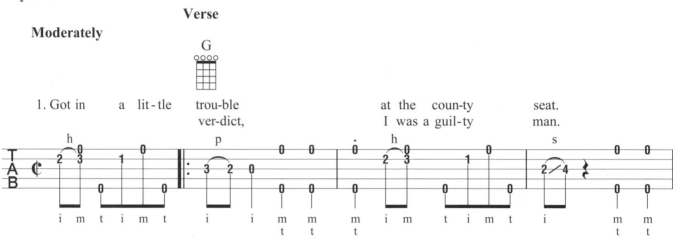

1. Got in a lit-tle trou-ble at the coun-ty seat.
   ver-dict, I was a guil-ty man.

Lord, they put me in the jail - house for loaf-ing on the street.
He said, "Fort-y-five dol - lars, or thir-ty days in the can."

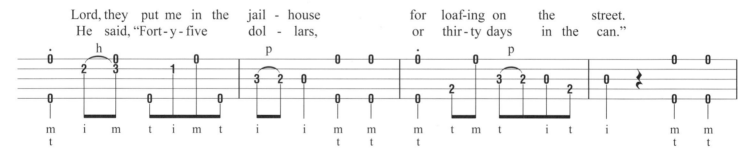

[1.] [2.]

Chorus

When the judge heard the / That-'ll be cash

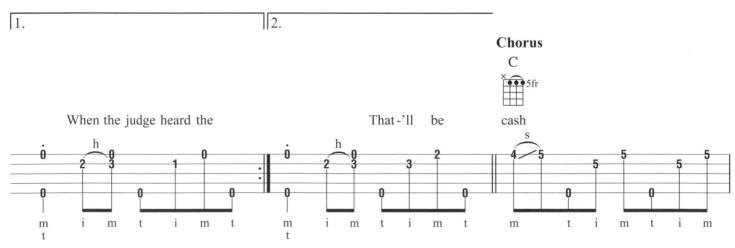

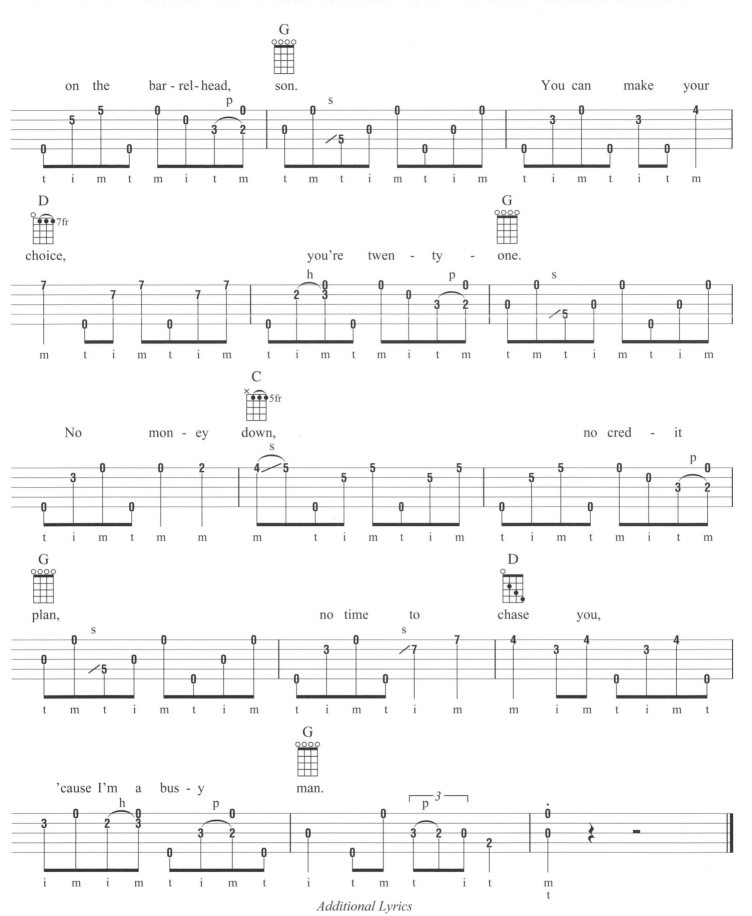

Additional Lyrics

2. Found a telephone number on a laundry slip.
   I had a good-hearted jailer with a six-gun hip.
   He let me call long distance. She said "Number, please."
   And no sooner than I told her, she shouted out at me:

Chorus: "That'll be cash on the barrelhead, son,
   Not part, not half, but the entire sum.
   No money down, no credit plan,
   'Cause a little bird tells me you're a travelin' man."

3. Thirty days in the jailhouse, four days on the road.
   I was feeling mighty hungry, my feet a heavy load.
   Saw a Greyhound coming, stuck out my thumb.
   Just as I was being seated, the driver caught my arm.

Chorus: That'll be cash on the barrelhead, son.
   This old "Grey Dog" is paid to run.
   When the engine stops, the wheels won't roll.
   Give me cash on the barrelhead,
   I'll take you down the road.

Clinch Mountain Backstep

Words and Music by Ralph Stanley and Carter Stanley

This instrumental was composed by Ralph Stanley, banjo player and singer for one of the first bluegrass groups, the Stanley Brothers and the Clinch Mountain Boys. He developed it by re-working an old fiddle tune by John Morgan Salyer called "Lonesome John." The Stanleys began their career in 1946, and after Ralph's brother (Carter) died in 1966, Ralph carried on with his own group and became one of the most renowned bluegrass singers of all time. The tune is based on a bluesy scale that includes flatted thirds and sevenths (no major thirds!), and the B part features a bar of 6/4 time (two extra beats). This arrangement duplicates what Ralph played on the original 1959 recording of the tune. The band played in G#, so Ralph was either tuned up a half step, or capoed on the first fret with the fifth string tuned to G#.

G tuning:
(5th-1st) G-D-G-B-D

Key of G

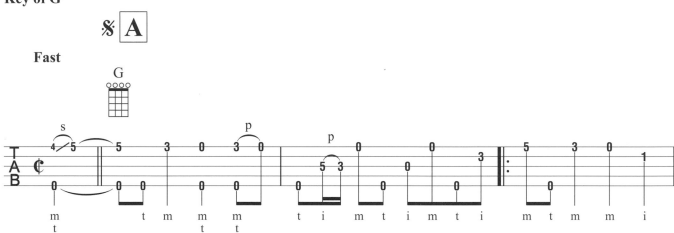

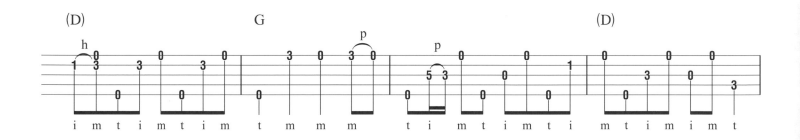

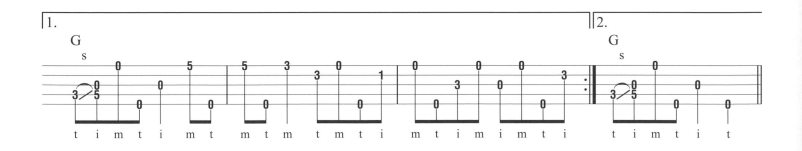

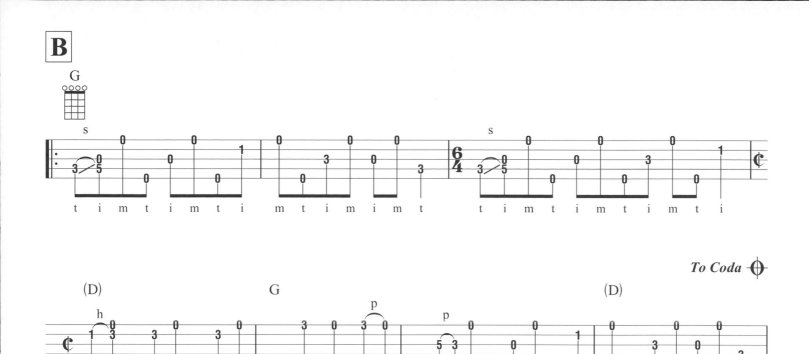

To Coda ⊕

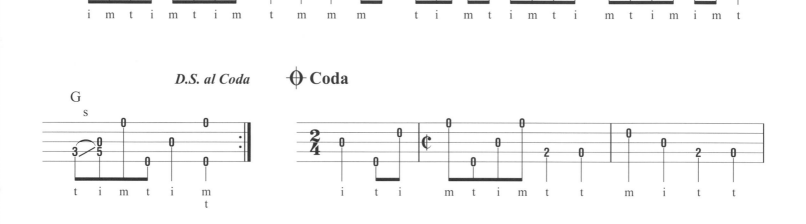

D.S. al Coda ⊕ **Coda**

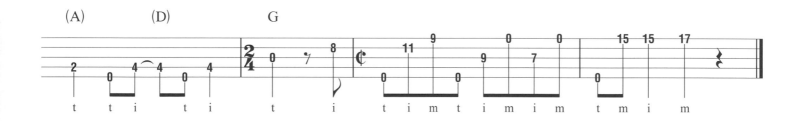

Cripple Creek

American Fiddle Tune

There's a Cripple Creek in Virginia and one in Colorado, and this key-of-A fiddle tune could refer to either one. The melody is well over a century old and words were put to it in the early 1900s, but bluegrassers play it as an instrumental. Popularized by Earl Scruggs, it's one of the first solos most bluegrass banjoists learn. The second time around the AABB format features a melodic approach to the tune. Since this arrangement is in G, you might want to capo up two frets and tune the fifth string to A, in case you want to play the song with a fiddler!

G tuning:
(5th-1st) G-D-G-B-D

Key of G

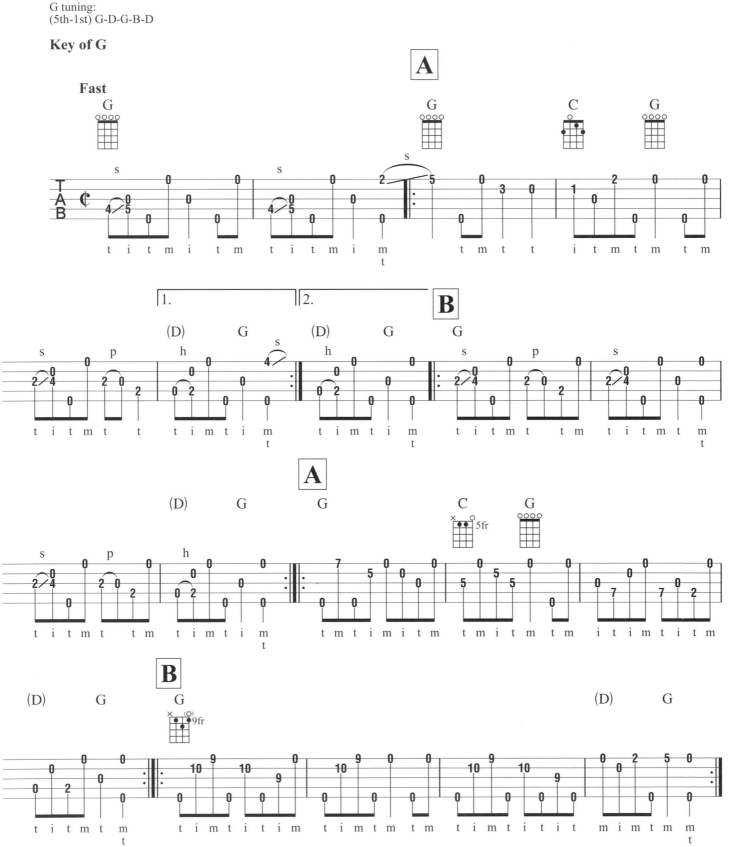

Dark Hollow

Traditional

When the Grateful Dead began playing this song in the early 1970s, it had already been a bluegrass standard for over a decade, due to recordings by Mac Wiseman, and others. The verse and chorus share the same melody.

G tuning:
(5th-1st) G-D-G-B-D

Key of G

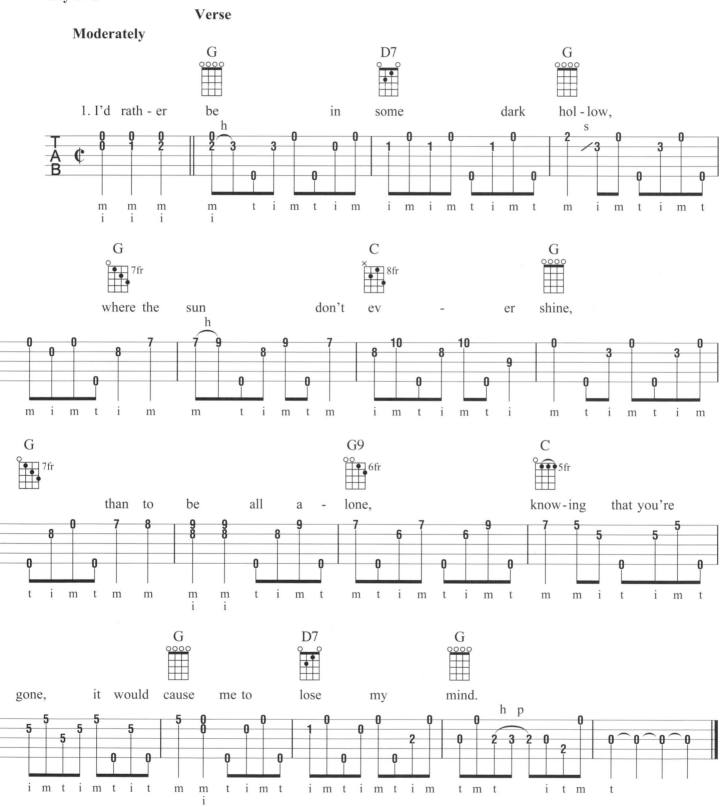

Down in the Willow Garden

Traditional

Sometimes called "Rose Connelly," this murder ballad probably originated in Ireland in the early 1800s, and folk song collector Cecil Sharp heard it in Appalachia as early as 1918. Charlie Monroe recorded it in 1947, and it became a bluegrass standard. There are versions by the Stanley Brothers, Flatt and Scruggs, the Osborne Brothers, Bill Monroe, Dan Tyminsky, Tim O'Brian and many others.

G tuning:
(5th-1st) G-D-G-B-D

Key of G

Verse

Moderately

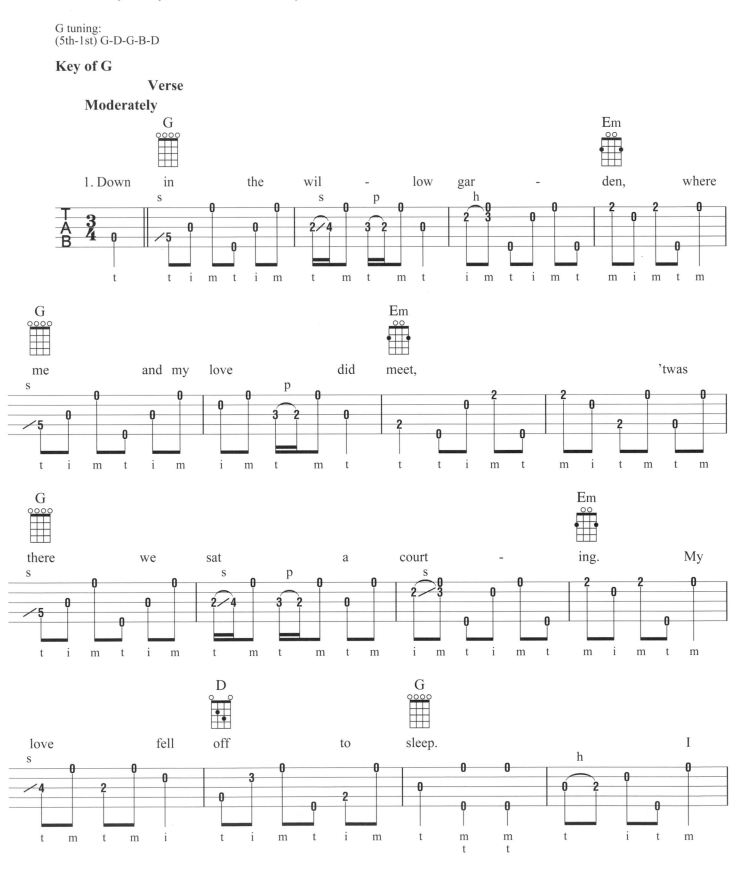

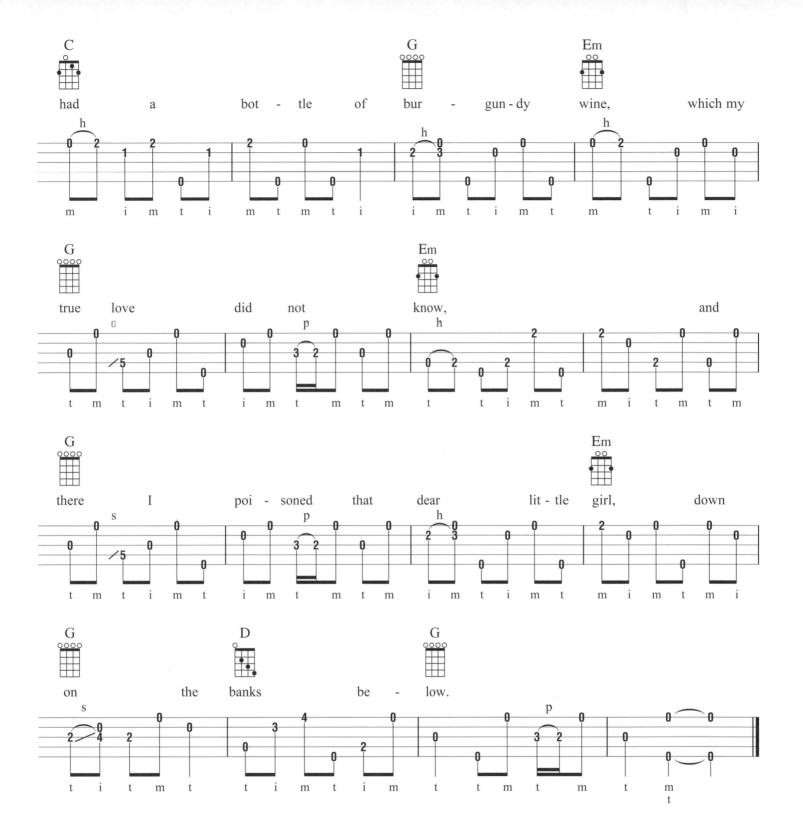

Additional Lyrics

2. I drew my saber through her which was a bloody knife.
   I threw her in the river, which was an awful sight.
   My father often told me that money would set me free,
   If I would murder that dear little miss whose name was Rose Connelly.

3. Now he sits by his cabin door a wiping his tear-brimmed eyes,
   Mourning for his only son out on the scaffold high.
   My race is run beneath the sun, the devil is waiting for me,
   For I did murder that dear little girl whose name was Rose Connelly.

Down the Road

By Lester Flatt and Earl Scruggs

Lester Flatt wrote "Down the Road," and it appeared on Flatt and Scruggs' 1958 Mercury Lp, *Country Music*. Notice the odd bar of 2/4 time at the end of the verse. Scruggs played several solos, and the following arrangement is his first solo. The second, up-the-neck version is what he played while Lester Flatt sang the third verse. It's a great example of Scruggs' brilliant accompaniment style. They played the song in the key of B, so if you want to duplicate the recorded version, capo up four frets and tune the fifth string to B.

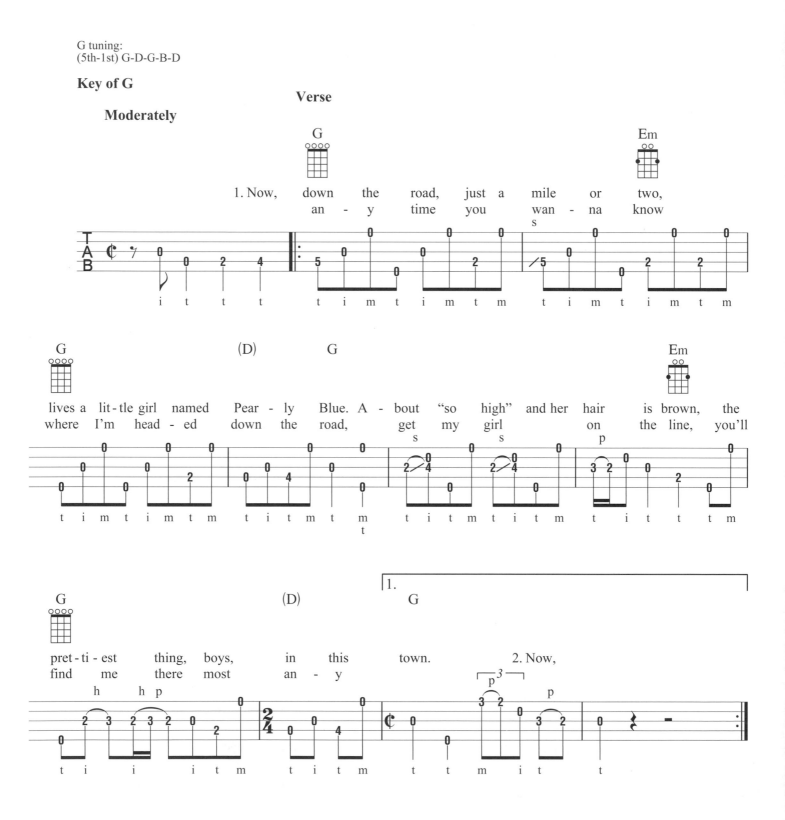

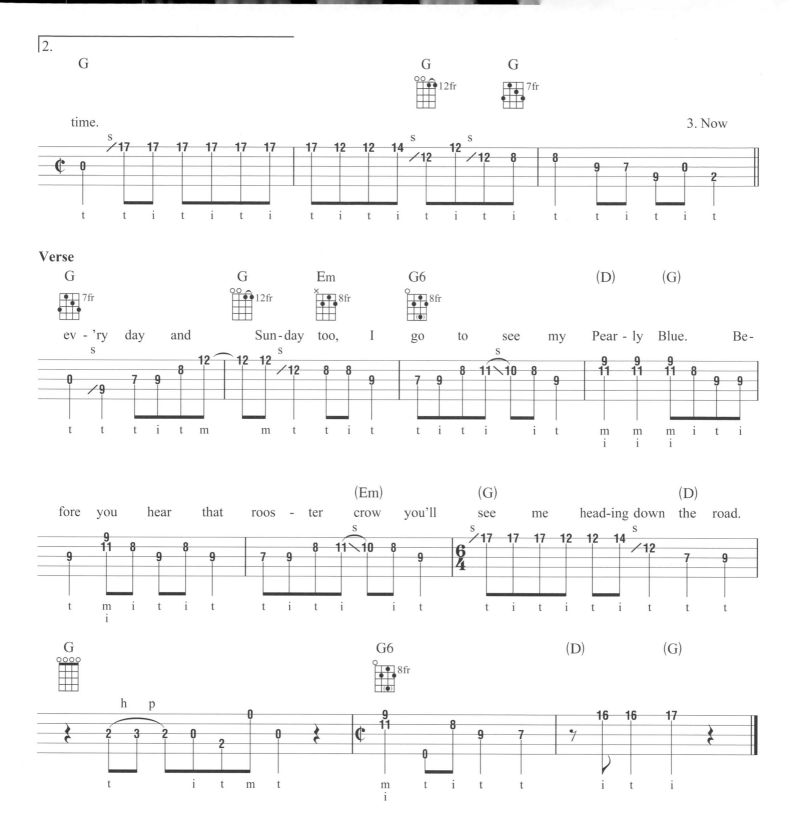

Additional Lyrics

4. Now, old man Flatt, he owned the farm
   From the hog lot to the barn.
   From the barn to the rail,
   He made his living by carrying the mail.

5. Now, every time I get the blues,
   I walk the soles right off my shoes.
   I don't know why I love her so,
   That gal of mine lives down the road.

Duelin' Banjos

By Arthur Smith

Arthur "Guitar Boogie" Smith, prolific songwriter/producer/multi-instrumentalist, wrote "Feudin' Banjos" in 1954, but when banjoist Eric Weissberg and guitarist Steve Mandell recorded it for the *Deliverance* movie (1972), they called it "Duelin' Banjos." Their version is one of the few bluegrass tunes to score high on the pop charts, and it sparked a good deal of interest in bluegrass banjo among the general population. The "duel" consists of the banjo answering the guitar licks. Below, you'll find the introductory "duel," and Weissberg's first solo…plus the colorful, extended ending of his second solo. The recording is in the key of A, he's capoed up two frets and his fifth string is tuned up to A.

G tuning:
(5th-1st) G-D-G-B-D

Key of G

Rubato

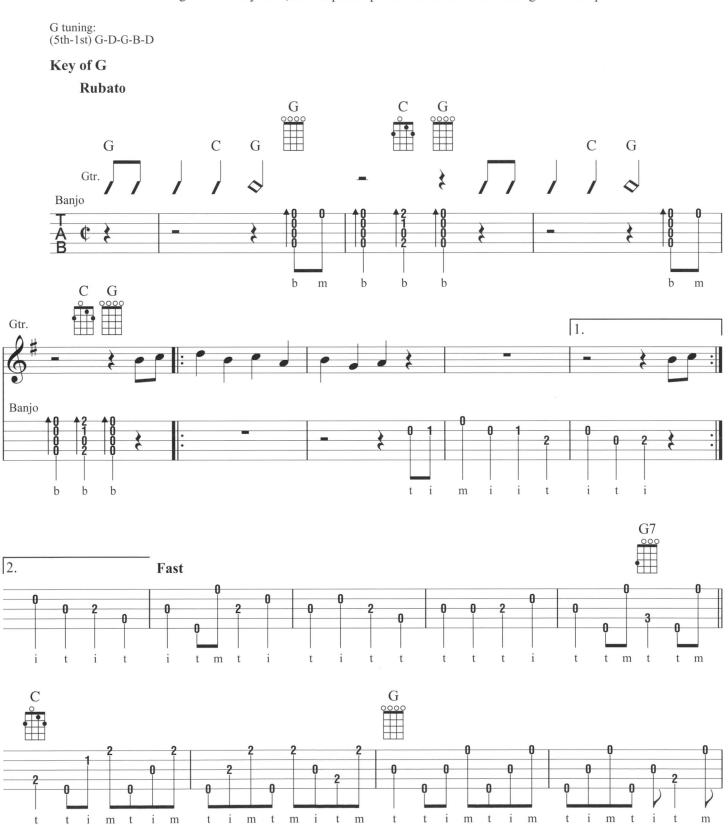

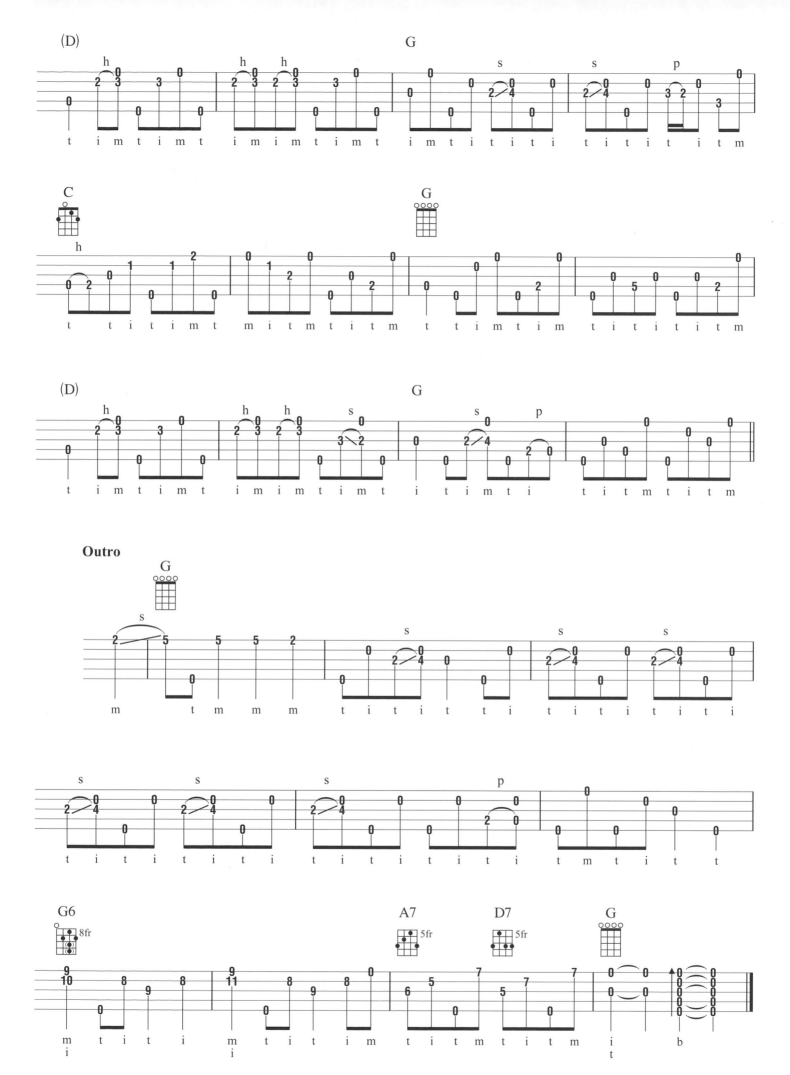

Foggy Mountain Breakdown

By Earl Scruggs

In the bluegrass world, fast instrumentals are often called "breakdowns." In 1949, Earl Scruggs wrote what is arguably the most popular banjo instrumental ever, "Foggy Mountain Breakdown," and he recorded it with Lester Flatt and the Foggy Mountain Boys. It had a second life in 1968 when it was featured in the movie *Bonnie and Clyde*. As it's the first bluegrass instrumental to achieve pop acclaim, learning to play it is a rite of passage for a bluegrass banjoist. For the record, Lester Flatt played an E major over Scruggs' E minor chord.

The arrangement below is from the 1949 recording; it's Scruggs' first solo and his up-the-neck solo that follows the first fiddle break. The band often tuned all their instruments up a half step on early recordings, so the 1949 recording is in G#, but everyone plays the tune in G.

G tuning:
(5th-1st) G-D-G-B-D

Key of G

Fast

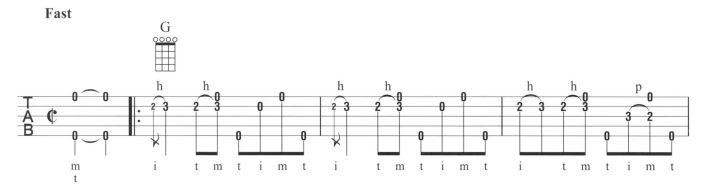

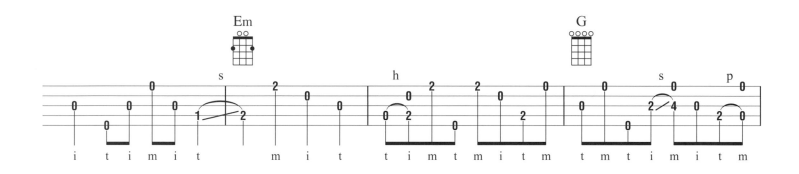

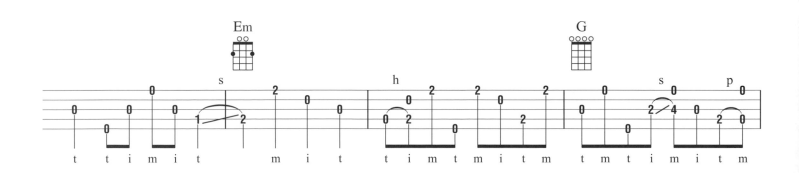

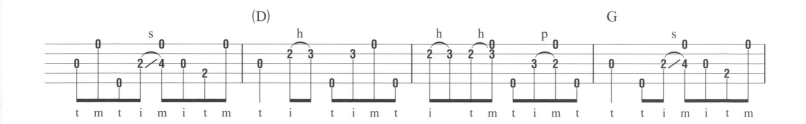

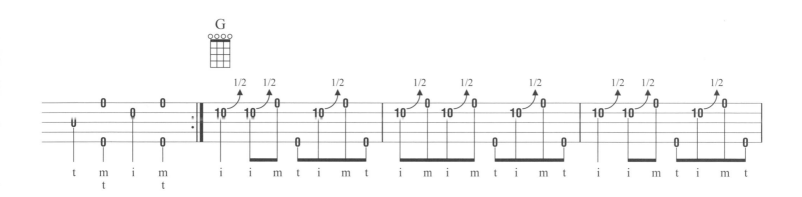

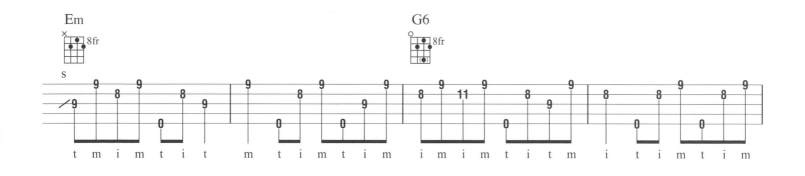

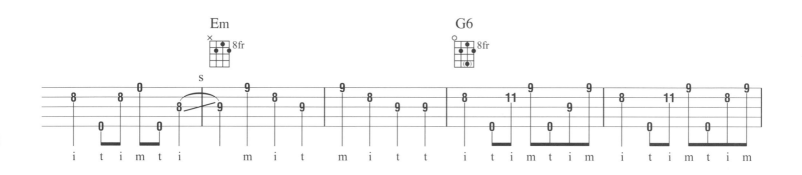

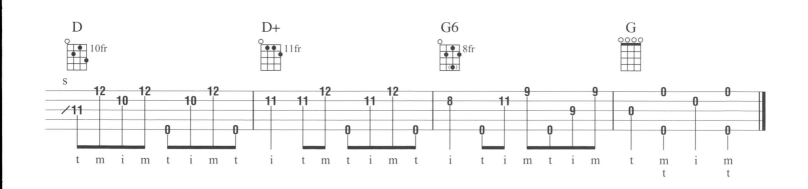

Fox on the Run

Words and Music by Tony Hazzard

First recorded by British rockers Manfred Mann in 1968, progressive bluegrassers Seldom Scene and the Country Gentlemen both brought "Fox on the Run" into the bluegrass orbit, where it became a favorite at bluegrass festivals during the 1970s. Neither Ben Eldridge of the Seldom Scene nor Eddie Adcock of the Country Gentlemen played a full verse/solo on their recordings or in performances, but you'll find one written below.

G tuning:
(5th-1st) G-D-G-B-D

Key of G

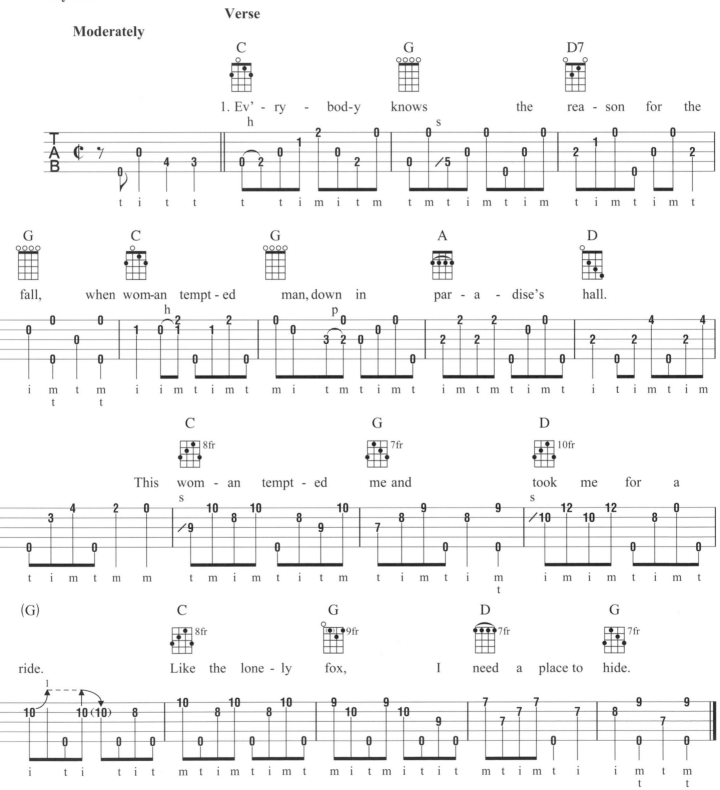

High on a Mountain Top

Words and Music by Ola Belle Reed

Songwriter/banjo player Ola Belle Reed wrote "High on a Mountain Top," a bluesy song that has that "high lonesome sound" that's a trademark of Appalachian and bluegrass music. It has been recorded by Del McCoury, Tim O'Brien and other bluegrass luminaries. The very imaginative, bluesy solo below is what Del McCoury's son Rob McCoury played on the 2009 *Del McCoury by Request* album.

G tuning:
(5th-1st) G-D-G-B-D

Key of G

Verse

Moderately

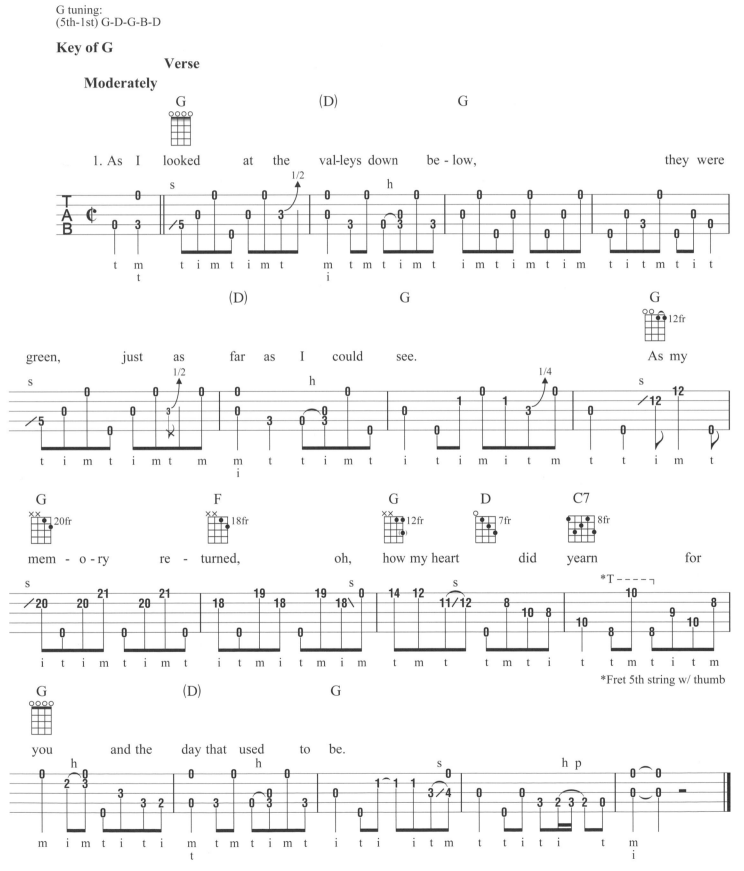

*Fret 5th string w/ thumb

How Mountain Girls Can Love

Words and Music by Carter Stanley

"How Mountain Girls Can Love" is one of the Stanley Brothers' most popular compositions. Both of Ralph Stanley's banjos breaks on the 1958 Stanley Brothers recordings are transcribed here. Notice how he played primarily index finger-lead forward rolls and played most of the melody notes with his index finger as well. The recording of the song is in A, so Ralph is capoed up two frets with his fifth string tuned to A.

G tuning:
(5th-1st) G-D-G-B-D

Key of G

Fast

Verse

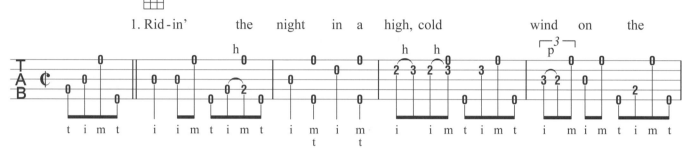

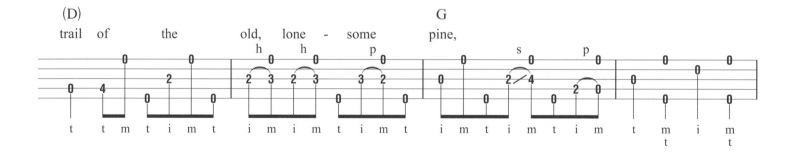

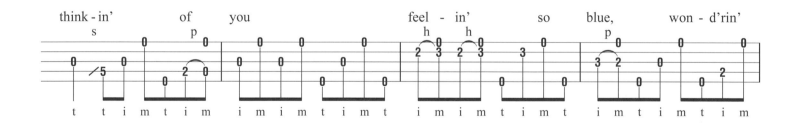

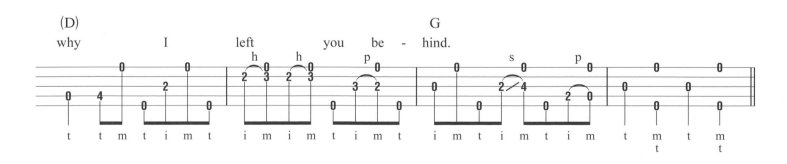

Verse

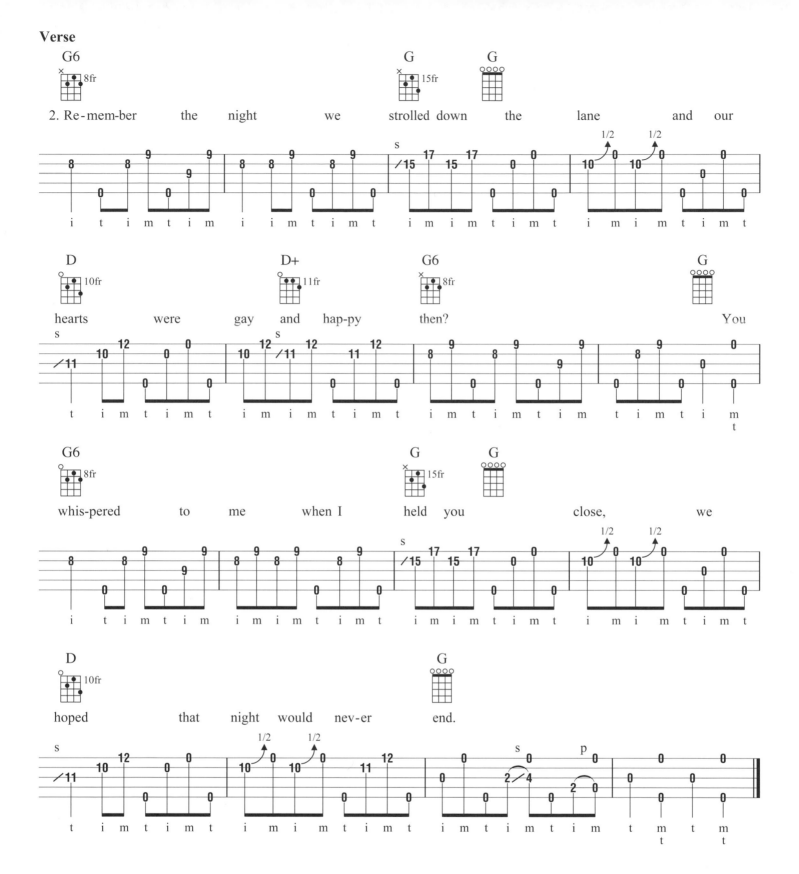

Additional Lyrics

Chorus: Get on, boys, go back home,
Back to the girl you love.
Treat her right, never wrong.
How mountain girls can love.

I Am a Man of Constant Sorrow

Words and Music by Carter Stanley and Ralph Stanley

"Man of Constant Sorrow" was published in a songbook in 1913, and Bob Dylan included it in his first (1962) recording. The Stanley Brothers' 1959 recording was the template for the version in the 2000 film, *O Brother, Where Art Thou?*, which became a million-selling hit. In the arrangement below, the first half of the verse is played in first position, the second half is played up the neck.

G tuning:
(5th-1st) G-D-G-B-D

Key of G

Moderately

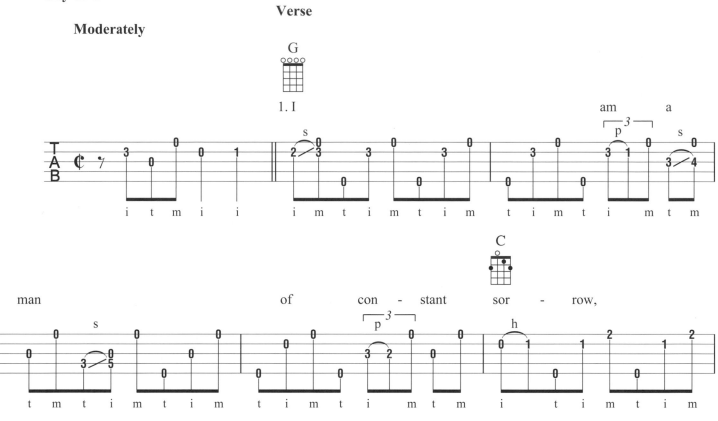

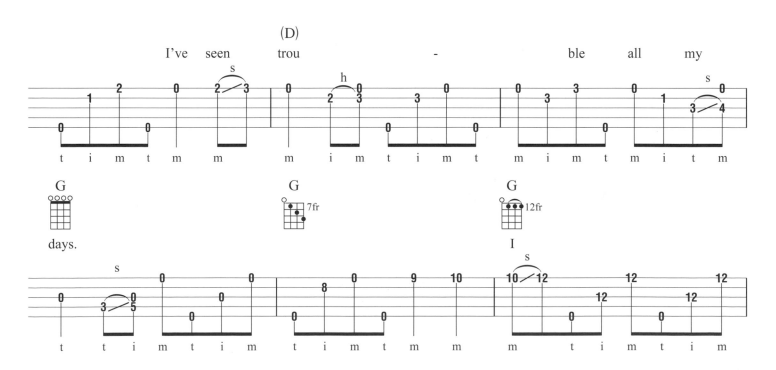

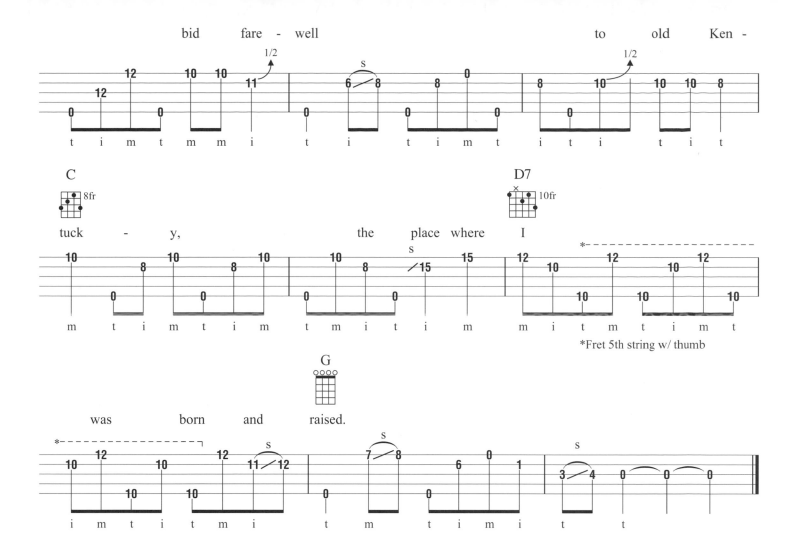

Additional Lyrics

2. For six long years I've been in trouble,
No pleasure here on earth I find.
For in this world I'm bound to ramble.
I have no friends to help me now.
He has no friends to help him now.

3. It's fare thee well, my own true lover.
I never expect to see you again.
For I'm bound to ride that northern railroad.
Perhaps I'll die upon this train.
Perhaps he'll die upon this train.

4. You can bury me in some deep valley,
For many years where I may lay.
Then you may learn to love another,
While I am sleeping in my grave.
While he is sleeping in his grave.

5. Maybe your friends think I'm just a stranger,
My face you never will see no more.
But there is one promise that is given:
I'll meet you on God's golden shore.
He'll meet you on God's golden shore.

I Wish You Knew

Words and Music by Charles Louvin and Ira Louvin

Bluegrass legends Jim and Jesse McReynolds and the Virginia Boys recorded several Louvin Brothers songs, including "I Wish You Knew." Their 1963 version of the tune featured Jesse's unique crosspicking on mandolin (it sounds like fingerpicking) that spawned a crosspicking guitar style often called "McReynolds picking." Jim and Jesse's excellent banjo player, Allen Shelton, played the solo (on the chorus of the tune) that is transcribed below. The up-the-neck verse solo is the author's arrangement. The recording is in the key of B, so Shelton was capoed at the 4th fret with his fifth string tuned to B.

G tuning:
(5th–1st) G-D-G-B-D

Key of G

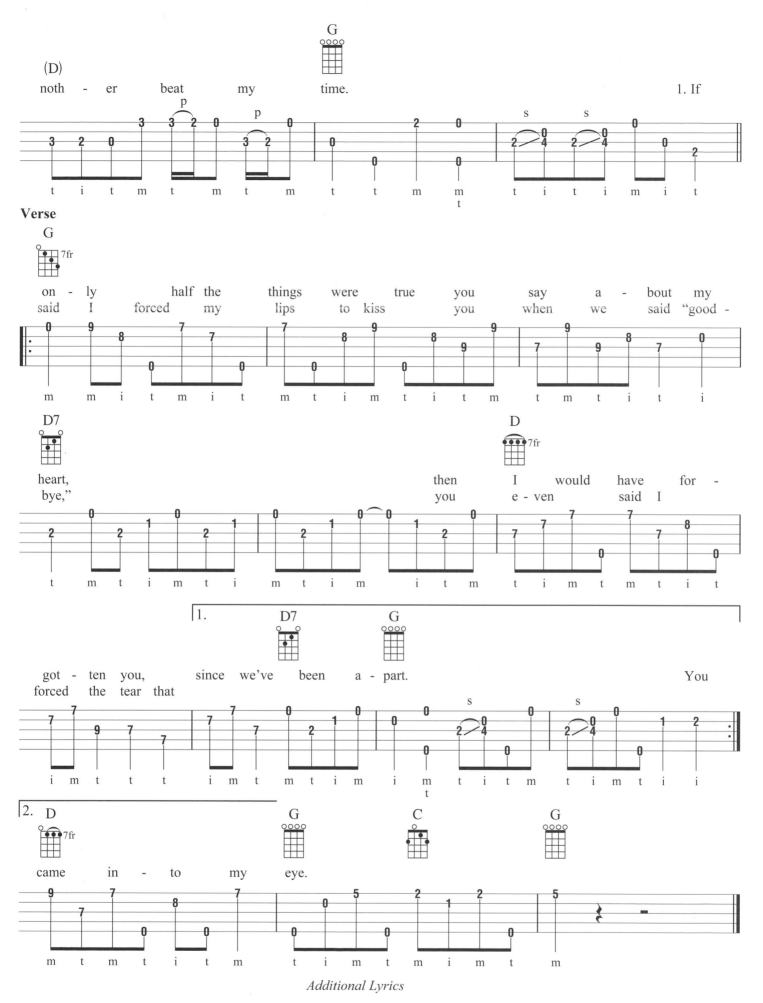

Additional Lyrics

2. There's not a thought that could be worse than knowing that you're gone,
   But in the picture in your mind, I'm never all alone.
   You see me in another's arms just like I was with you,
   And the way I cried for you each night, I almost wish you knew.

I Wonder Where You Are Tonight

Words and Music by Johnny Bond

This tune is a standard in country music as well as bluegrass, having been recorded by Hank Snow, Ernest Tubb and numerous other country legends. (It's often referred to by bluegrassers as "I'll Wear Your Underwear Tonight.") The first solo, below, is what Earl Scruggs played on Flatt and Scruggs' 1963 album, *Recorded Live at Carnegie Hall!* The song is played in E, so Earl tuned the fifth string up to G♯ and played without a capo. He often played in E this way: he didn't have to reach for a capo during a live performance, and he didn't lose the low notes of the banjo. In this Carnegie Hall show, he only played the second half of each solo, so the first halves are the author's arrangement.

Tuning:
(5th-1st) G♯-D-G-B-D

Key of E

Moderately

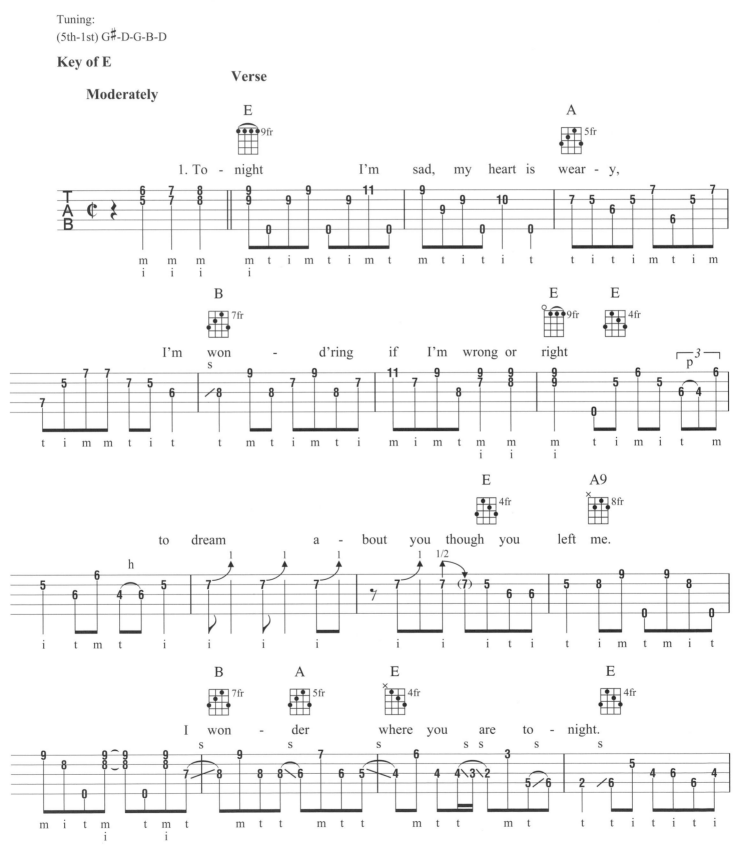

Verse

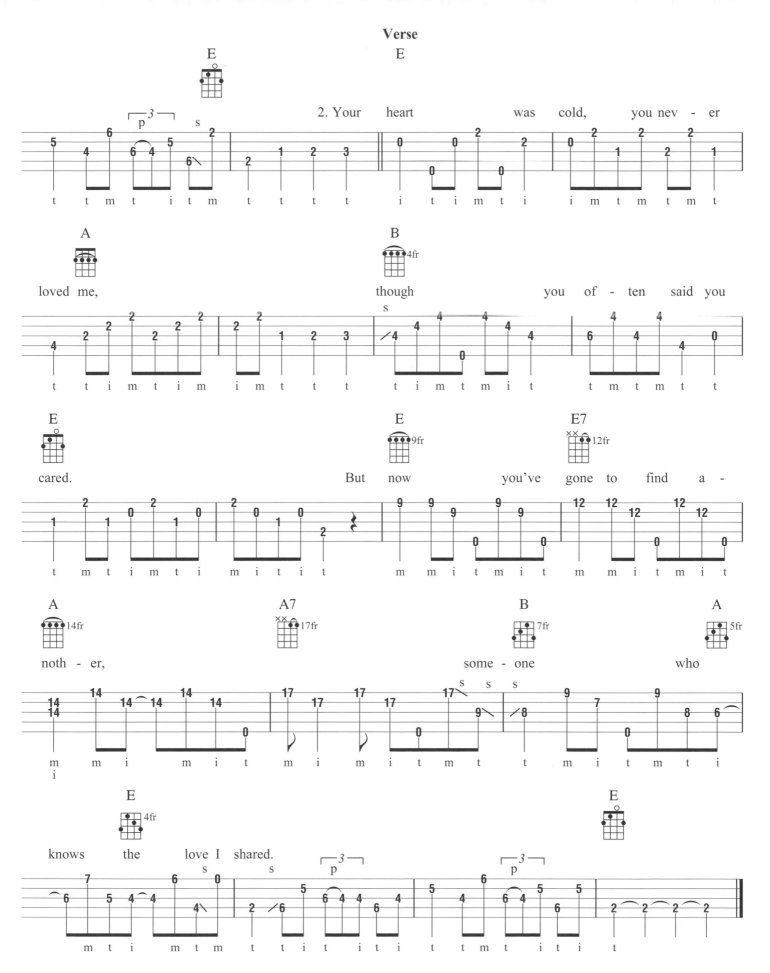

Additional Lyrics

3. Then came the dawn the day you left me,
I tried to smile with all my might.
But you could see the pain within me
That lingers in my heart tonight.

I'll Fly Away

Words and Music by Albert E. Brumley

Possibly the most recorded gospel song of all time (and not just in the bluegrass world), "I'll Fly Away" goes back to the 1920s. Its inclusion in the 2000 film *O Brother, Where Art Thou?* gave it new life and inspired subsequent recordings by many more artists. This version is a good example of bluegrass banjo picking in the key of C.

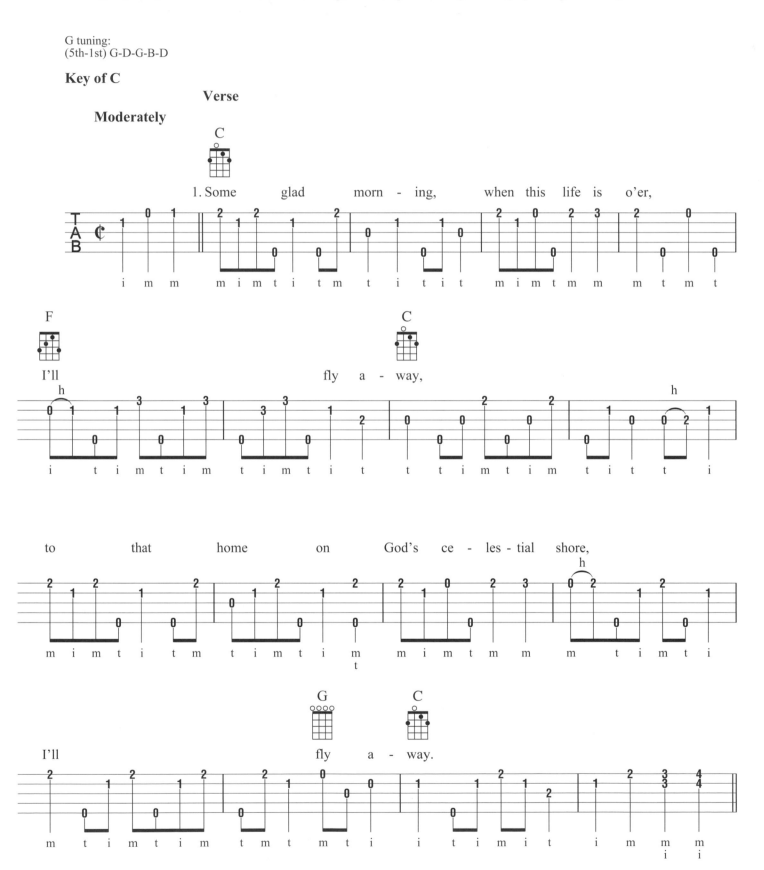

Chorus

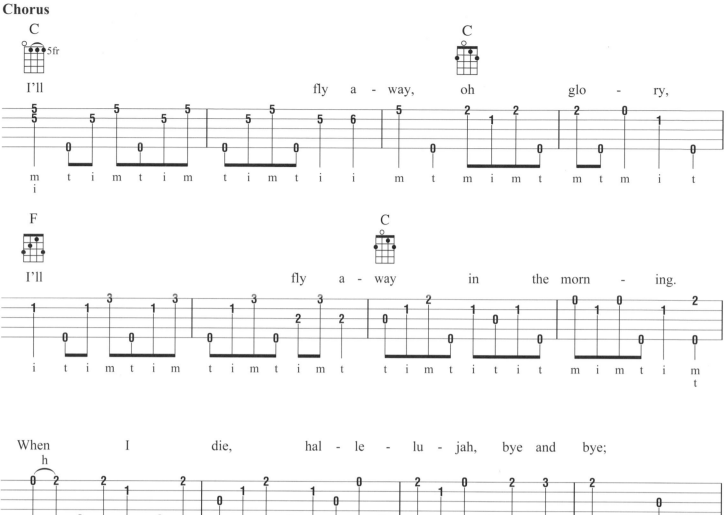

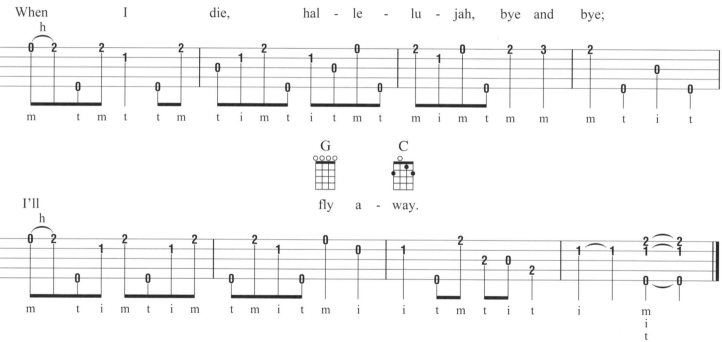

Additional Lyrics

2. When the shadows of this life have grown, I'll fly away.
   Like a bird from prison walls has flown, I'll fly away.

3. Oh, how glad and happy when we meet, I'll fly away.
   No more cold iron shackles on my feet, I'll fly away.

4. Just a few more weary days and then, I'll fly away.
   To a land where joys will never end, I'll fly away.

I'm Goin' Back to Old Kentucky

Words and Music by Bill Monroe

In 1948, "I'm Going Back to Old Kentucky" was the flip side of the single "Molly and Tenbrooks." These were the last songs Bill Monroe recorded when Flatt and Scruggs were in his band…the first band to be called a "bluegrass" band, and the ensemble whose style of music was imitated by all future bluegrass bands. The first solo, below, is what Scruggs played. The recording was in the key of A, so he was capoed on the second fret with his fifth string tuned to A. The second solo demonstrates how to play the tune in the key of C.

G tuning:
(5th-1st) G-D-G-B-D

Key of G

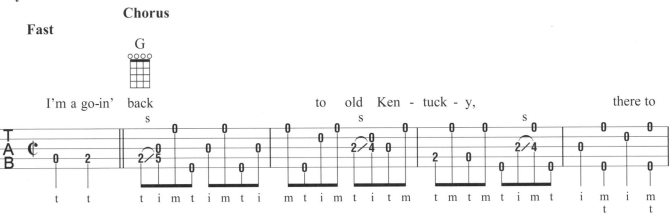

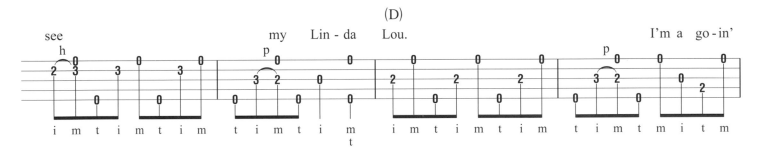

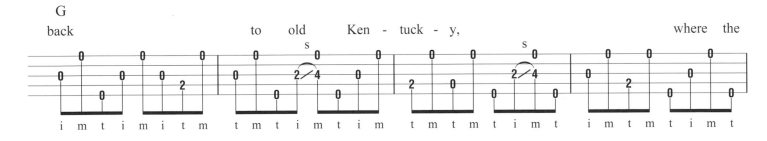

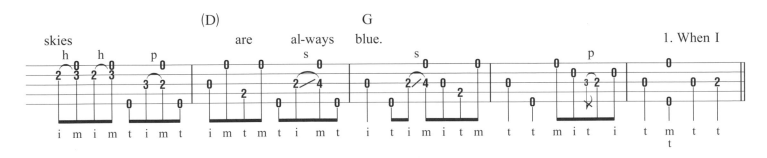

Verse

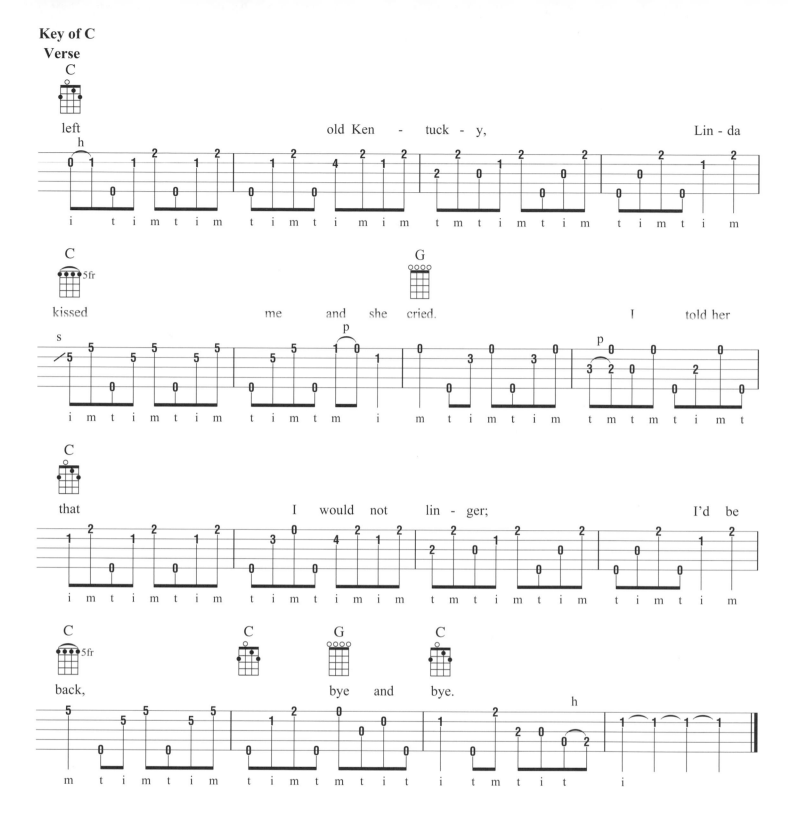

Additional Lyrics

2. Linda Lou, she is a beauty,
   Those pretty brown eyes I loved so well.
   I'm going back to old Kentucky,
   Never more to say farewell.

3. Linda Lou, you know I love you.
   I long for you each night and day.
   When the roses bloom in old Kentucky,
   I'll be coming back to stay.

If I Lose

Words and Music by Ralph Stanley

Written by Ralph Stanley, "If I Lose" was released in 1961 as a Stanley Brothers' 45 rpm single. It has become a staple in the repertoire of many a bluegrass band. The 1961 recording did not include a banjo solo because a guitarist took all the instrumental breaks. Usually the guitar plays the first half of the chorus and other instruments take turns playing the second half. In the version below, the second half of the chorus is what Ralph played on a 1998 *Ralph Stanley and Friends* album. He was in the key of B, capoed up four frets, with the fifth string tuned to B. The verse is the author's arrangement, played Ralph Stanley-style.

G tuning:
(5th-1st) G-D-G-B-D

Key of G

Moderately

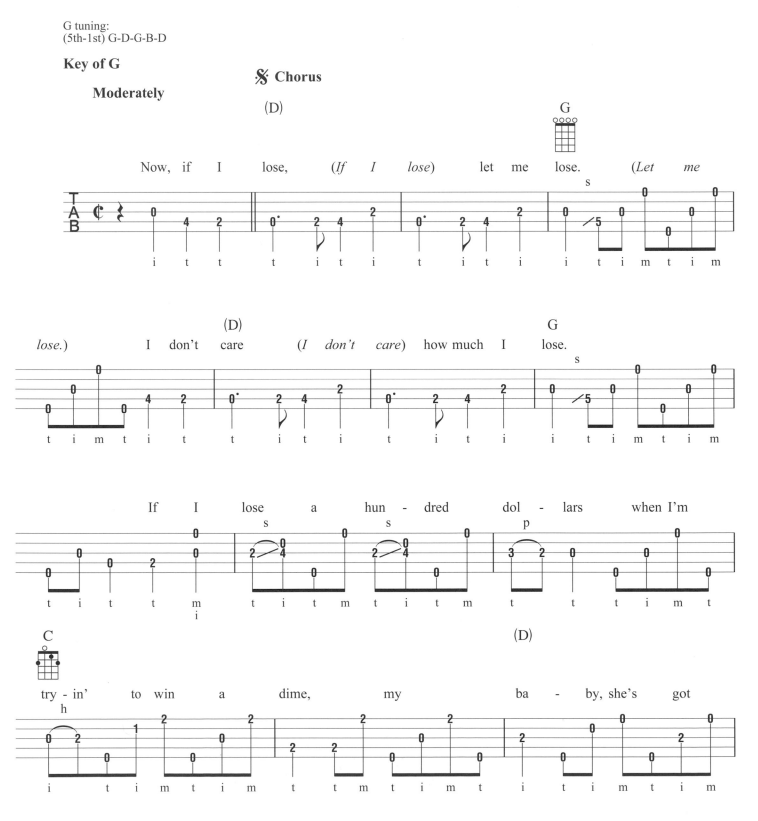

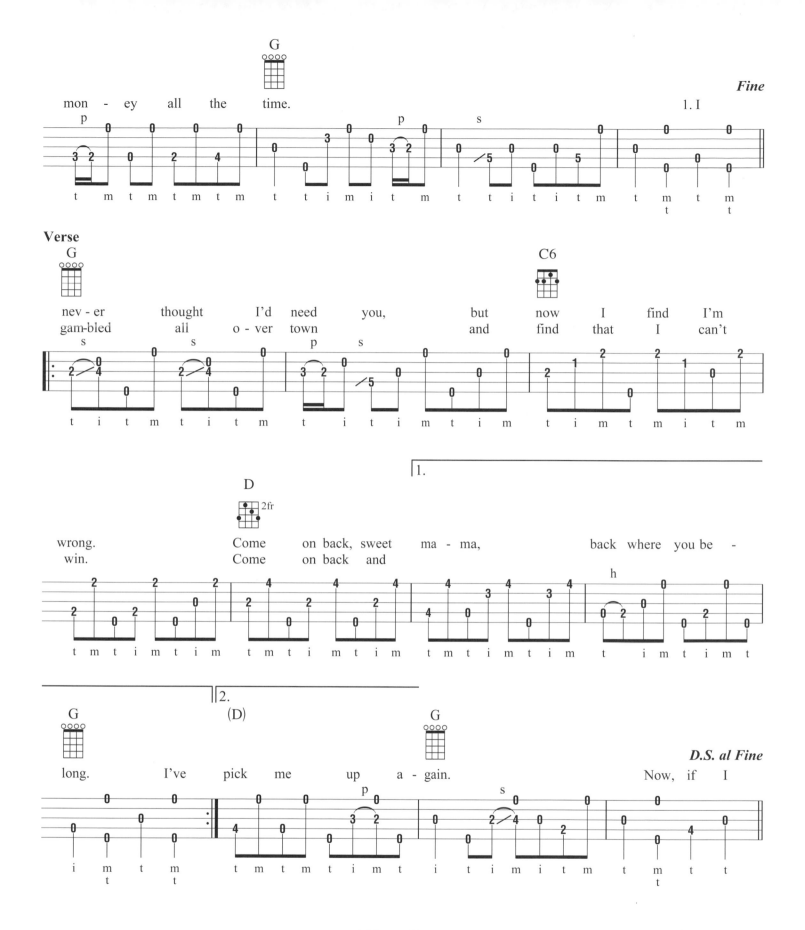

Additional Lyrics

2. Of all the other gals I know, none can take your place,
'Cause when I get into a jam, they just ain't in the race.
So now that you're back again, let's made another round.
With you here by my side, babe, the deal just can't go down.

In the Pines

Words and Music by Thomas Bryant, Jimmie Davis and Clayton McMichen

Nirvana performed Leadbelly's version of this old Appalachian folk song, but Bill Monroe's 1941 recording closely resembles a 1927 version by the Tenneva Ramblers, who started out as Jimmie Rodgers' backup band. Their version is called "The Longest Train." Monroe added a harmonized yodeling section. Many bluegrassers play his version.

The solo below shows how to play in the key of E with the fifth string tuned up to G♯ and no capo. You could also tune the fifth string to B. Notice all the triplets; the banjo can't sustain a note for long, but triplets are a good substitute when playing a ballad. The second half of the solo is in the style of Don Reno, one of the first bluegrass banjo players.

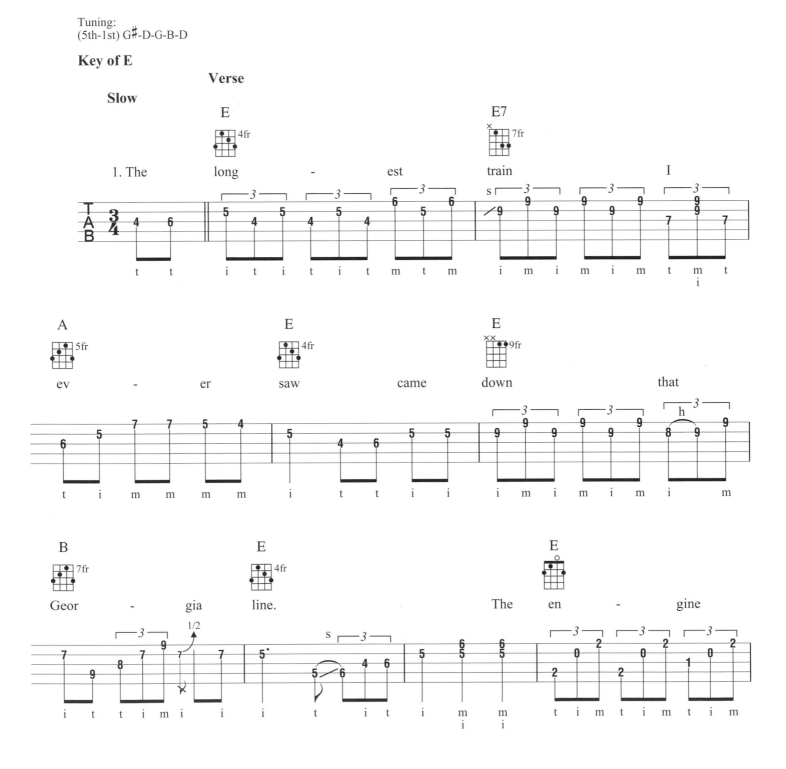

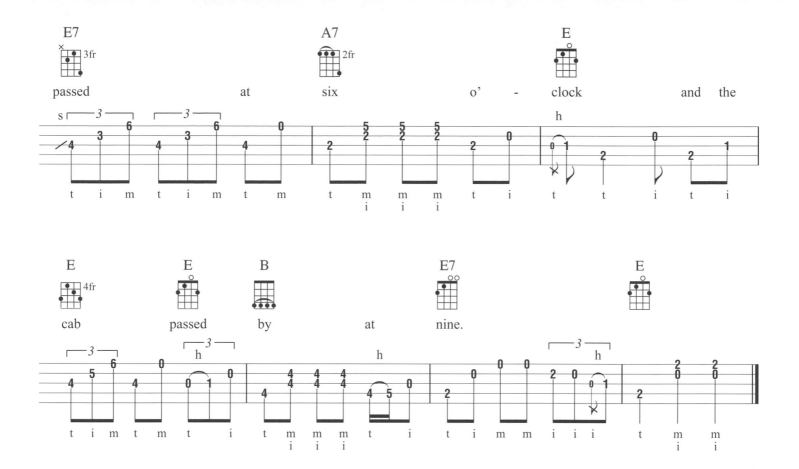

Additional Lyrics

2. I asked my captain for the time of day.
   He said he throwed his watch away.
   A long steel rail and a short cross tie,
   I'm on my way back home.

3. Little girl, little girl, what have I done
   That makes you treat me so?
   You caused me to weep, you caused me to mourn,
   You caused me to leave my home.

Keep on the Sunny Side

Words and Music by A.P. Carter

Written in 1899, this song was recorded by the Carter Family in 1928, and it eventually became their theme song. The song's composer, Ada Blenkhorn, got the title and idea for "Keep on the Sunny Side" from her disabled nephew, who always wanted his wheelchair pushed on the sunny side of the street.

G tuning:
(5th-1st) G-D-G-B-D

Key of G

Moderately

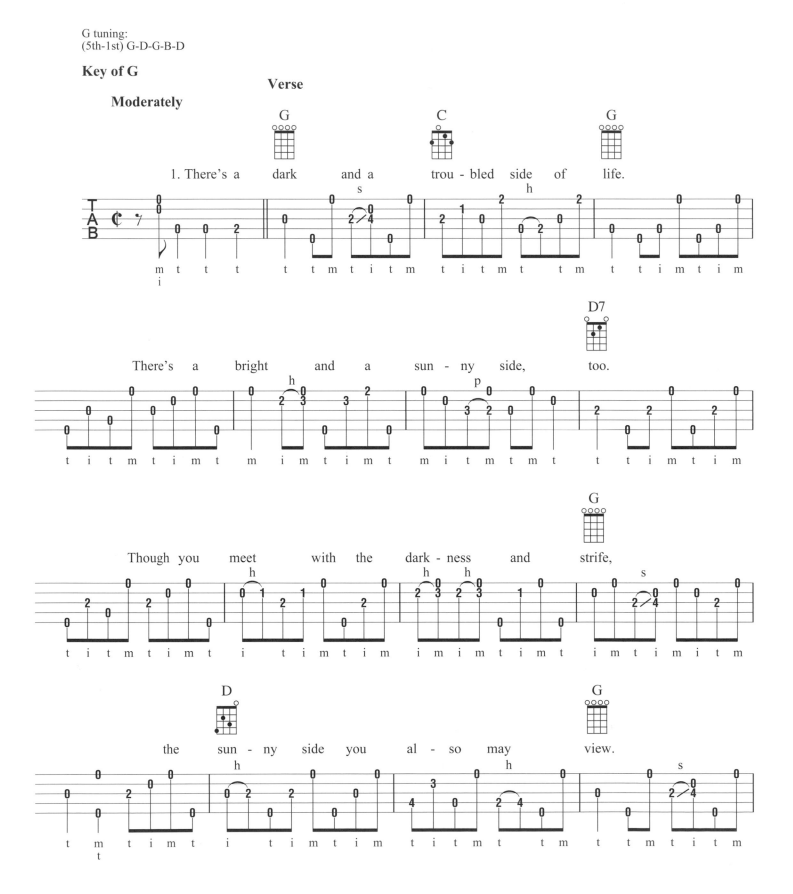

Chorus

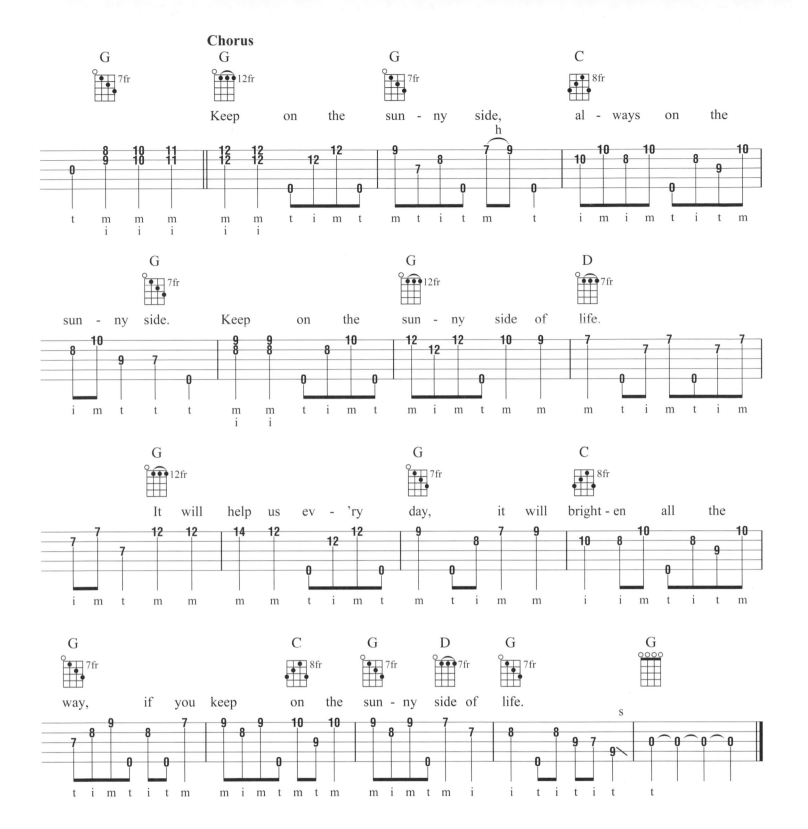

Additional Lyrics

2. Though a storm and its fury break today,
   Crushing hopes that we cherished so dear,
   Clouds and storm will in time pass away,
   The sun again will shine bright and clear.

3. Let us greet with a song of hope each day,
   Though the moment be cloudy or fair.
   Let us trust in our Savior always
   To keep us, everyone, in His care.

Little Cabin Home on the Hill

Words and Music by Lester Flatt and Bill Monroe

Bill Monroe recorded "Little Cabin Home on the Hill" in 1947, when his Bluegrass Boys included Flatt and Scruggs. The recordings made with that lineup are the original template for bluegrass. They played the song in the key of A, but Scruggs took no solo. Since the Monroe recording, there are versions by Ricky Skaggs, Tony Rice, Flatt and Scruggs, David Grisman, the Osborne Brothers and many others. Don't miss John Hartford's version, "Little Cabin Home on the Hill Waugh Waugh."

G tuning:
(5th-1st) G-D-G-B-D

Key of G

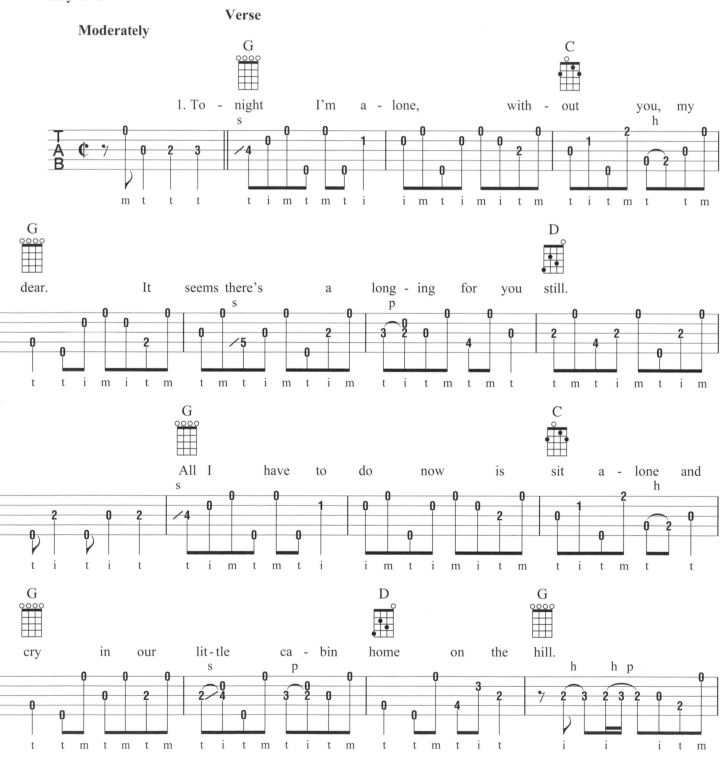

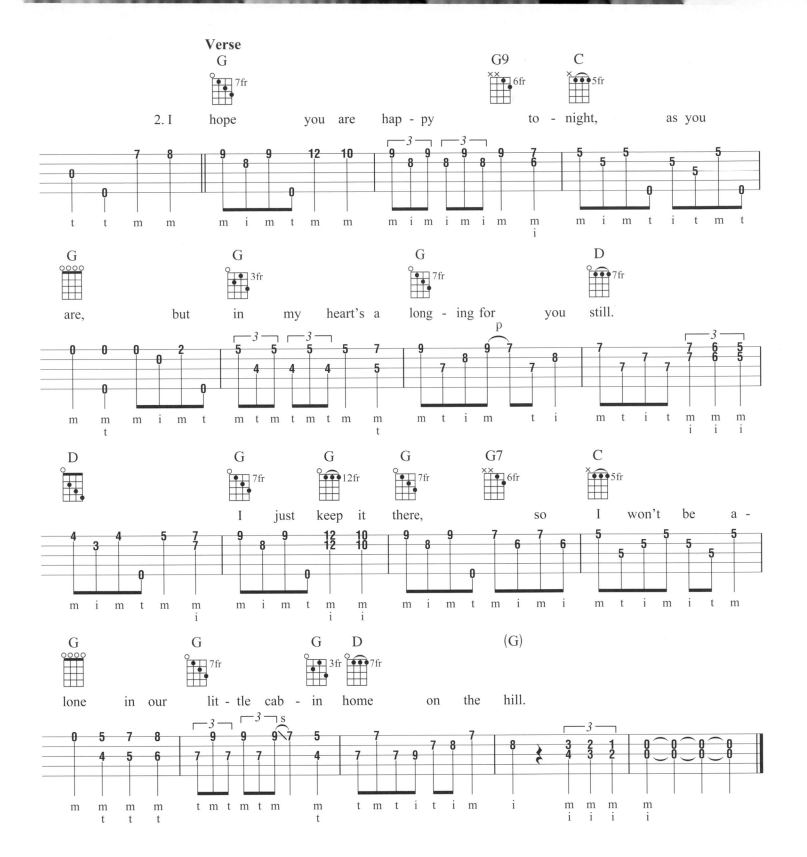

Additional Lyrics

3. Now when you have come to the end of the way,
   And find there's no more happiness for you,
   Just let your thoughts turn back once more, if you will,
   To our little cabin home on the hill.

Chorus: Oh, someone has taken you from me,
   And left me here all alone.
   Listen to the rain beat on our windowpane,
   In our little cabin home on the hill.

Little Maggie

Traditional

First recorded in 1930, "Little Maggie" is related to another old folk song about an outlaw woman, "Darling Corey." Both songs share the verse about the gal with a .44 pistol and a banjo (a dangerous combination). "Little Maggie" is one of the first recordings the Stanley Brothers made (in 1948).

G tuning:
(5th-1st) G-D-G-B-D

Key of G

Fast

Verse

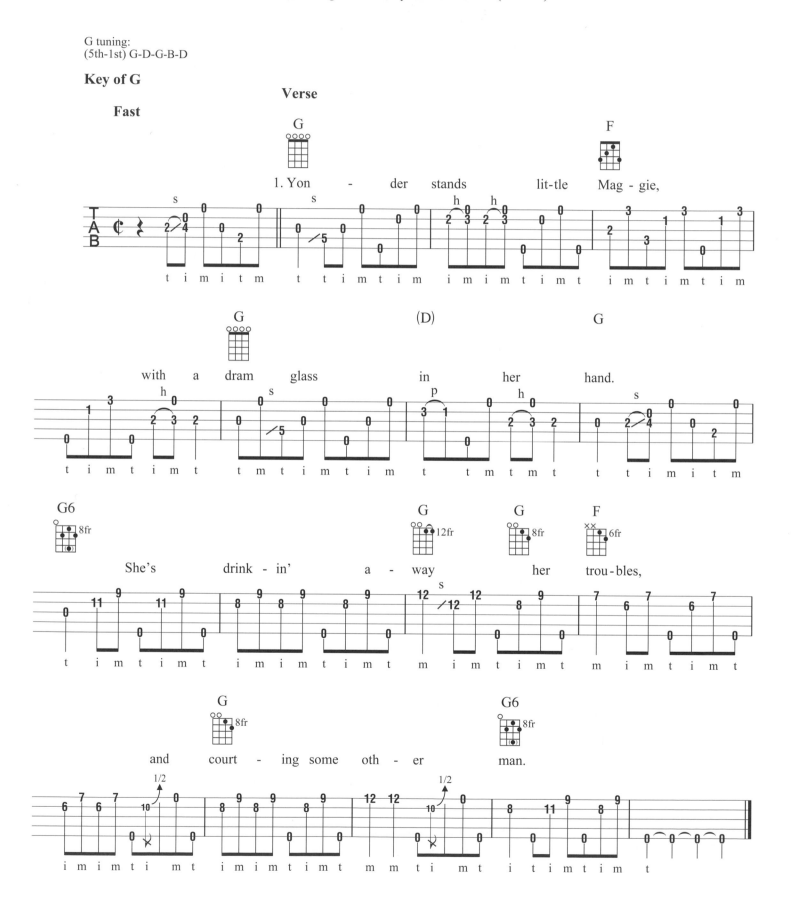

Rain and Snow

Traditional

Folk song collector Cecil Sharp notated a version of this Appalachian folk song in 1917. Many banjo players learned it from Obray Ramsey's 1961 recording of the tune…including bluegrass banjo picker, Jerry Garcia. The Grateful Dead's "Cold Rain and Snow," on their first album, is almost certainly based on Ramsey's recording. Though it's a rock interpretation, it brought the tune to the attention of the bluegrass community. In 1973, it was included on the bluegrass super-group, Old and in the Way's album *Muleskinner*, featuring Peter Rowan, Bill Keith, Clarence White, Richard Greene and David Grisman. Since then, it has been recorded or performed by Del McCoury, Chris Thile, Molly Tuttle and many others.

G tuning:
(5th-1st) G-D-G-B-D

Key of G

Moderately slow

Verse

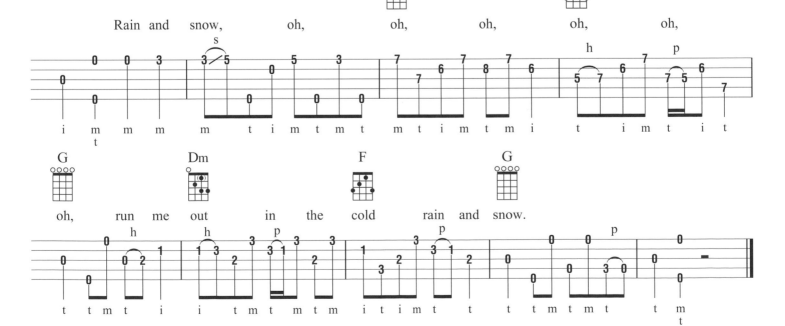

Love Please Come Home

Words and Music by Leon Jackson

This one was popularized by Reno and Smiley and the Tennessee Cutups, one of the first bluegrass groups. Don Reno was an innovative banjo player and prolific songwriter. He added "single string picking" to the Scruggs-style lexicon, a technique in which the thumb and index finger alternate, playing scale patterns that resemble flatpicking. He also performed a unique, triplet lick you'll find in the following solo to "Love Please Come Home." Both solos, below, are transcribed from Reno and Smiley's 1961 recording, which was in the key of A. The verses and chorus have the same melody and chord progression.

G tuning:
(5th-1st) G-D-G-B-D

Key of G

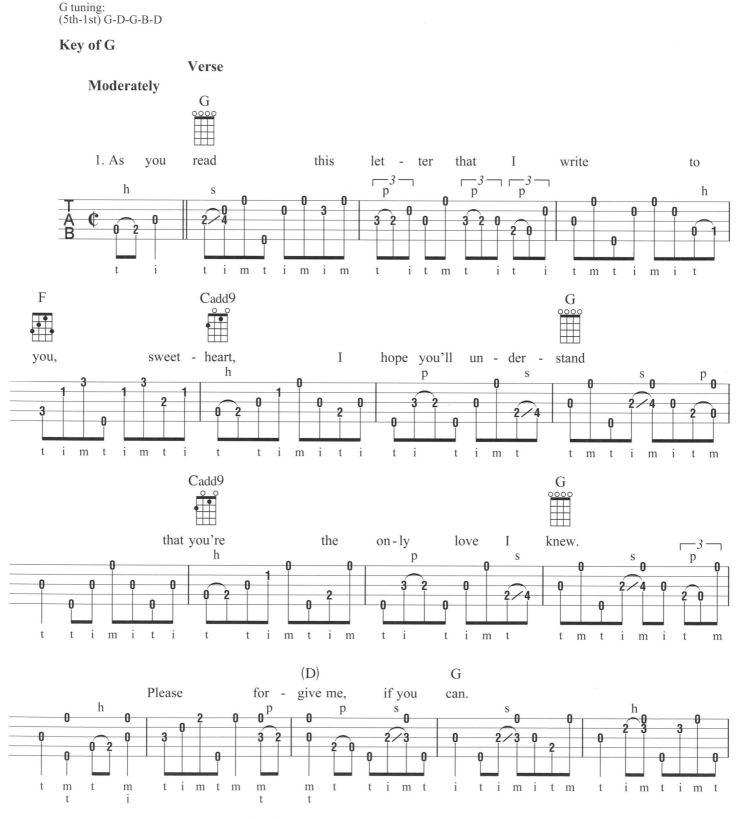

Chorus

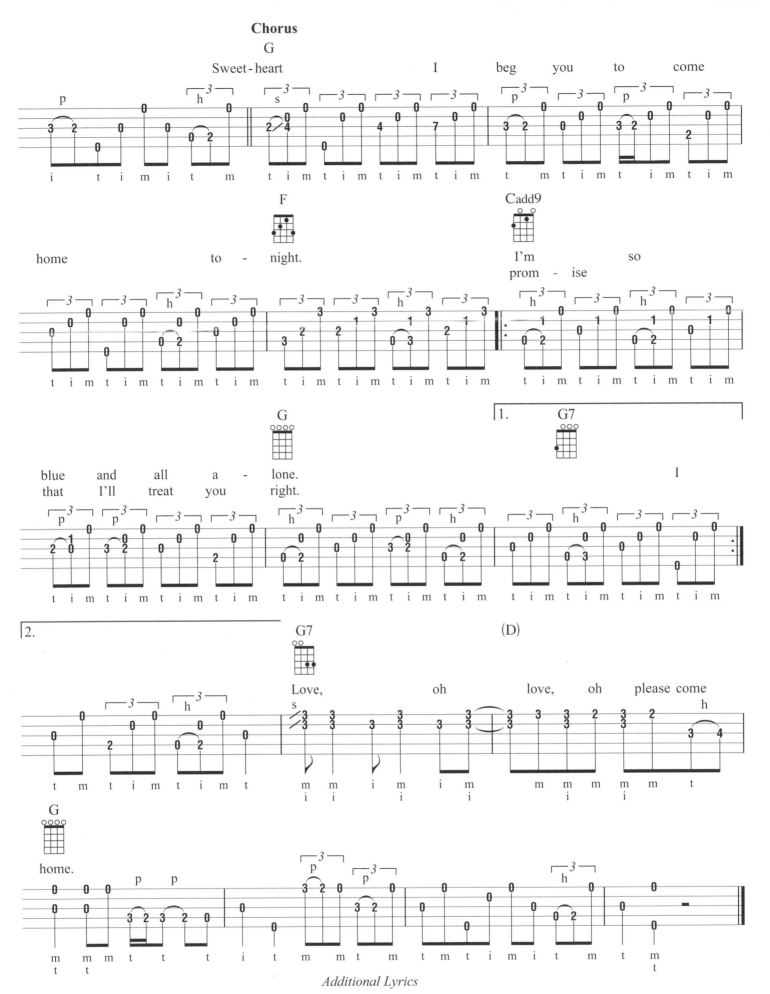

Midnight Moonlight

Words and Music by Peter Rowan

Bluegrass singer/songwriter/guitarist Peter Rowan, who was one of Bill Monroe's Bluegrass Boys for a year (late 1966–'67), introduced his "Midnight Moonlight" on the famous *Old and in the Way* album of 1975. One of the best-selling bluegrass albums of all time, the super group Old and in the Way consisted of Rowan, Jerry Garcia, David Grisman, Vassar Clements and John Kahn. The song has been performed by many bluegrass groups. Rather than soloing over the chord changes of the verse or chorus, the banjo and other instruments usually take turns soloing over four bars of C and four bars of A, over and over. The solo below is what Garcia played on the album. He was capoed at the 2nd fret, and that's why the tab below, written in respect to the capo, goes from B♭ to G, instead of C to A.

G tuning:
(5th-1st) G-D-G-B-D

Key of G

Intro

Moderately

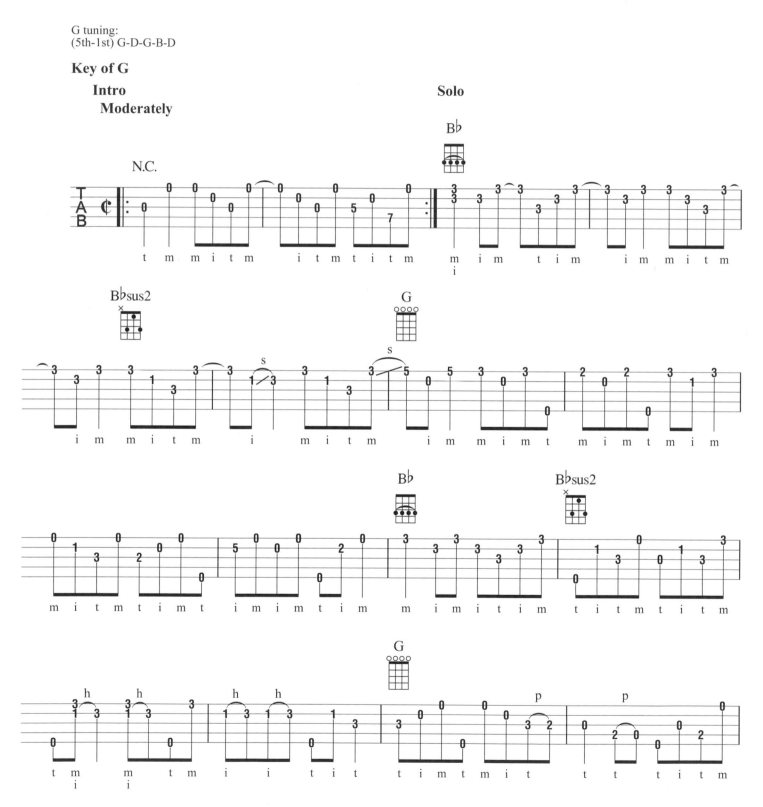

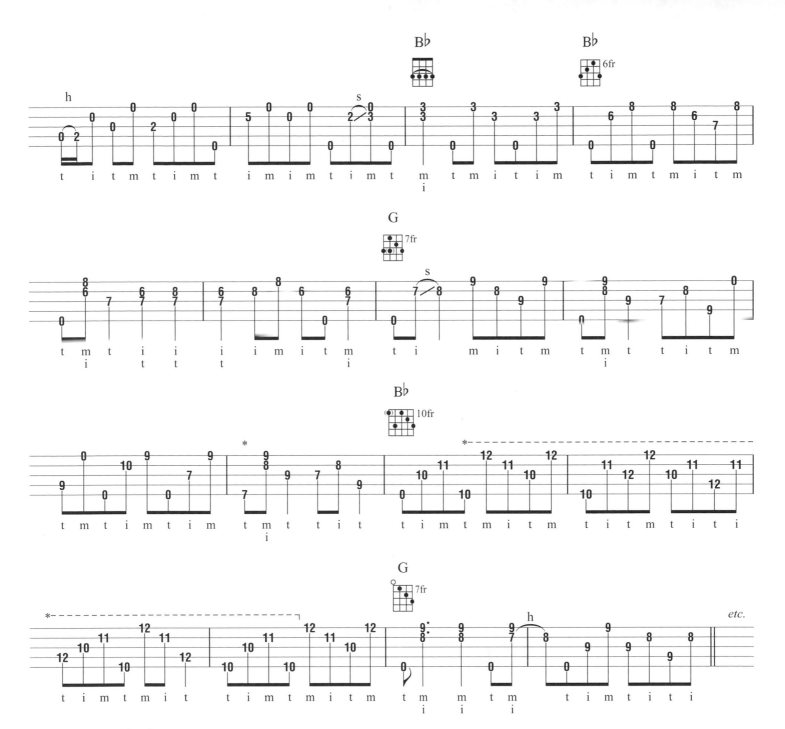

*Fret 5th string w/ thumb

Molly and Tenbrooks

Words and Music by Bill Monroe

A fictionalized song about an actual horse race that occurred in 1878, this tune was written shortly after the event, but the version that impacted the bluegrass world is Bill Monroe's 1947 recording. During Earl Scruggs' 1946 debut performance with Bill Monroe and His Bluegrass Boys at the Grand Ol' Opry, he caused a sensation with his solos on "Molly and Tenbrooks." The audience had never heard a banjo played like that, and they applauded and made him play it over and over…and banjo picking has never been the same since.

The music below is Scruggs' first solo on the 1947 Bill Monroe recording, which was in the key of B; the second solo shows how Scruggs might have played it up the neck. (To play in B, capo at the 4th fret and tune the fifth string to B.)

G tuning:
(5th-1st) G-D-G-B-D

Key of G

Fast

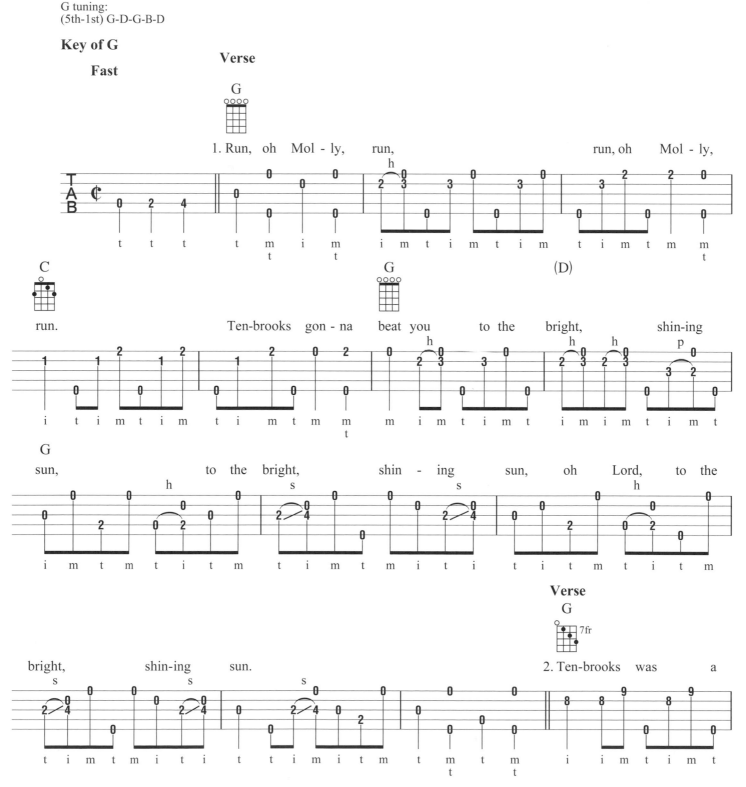

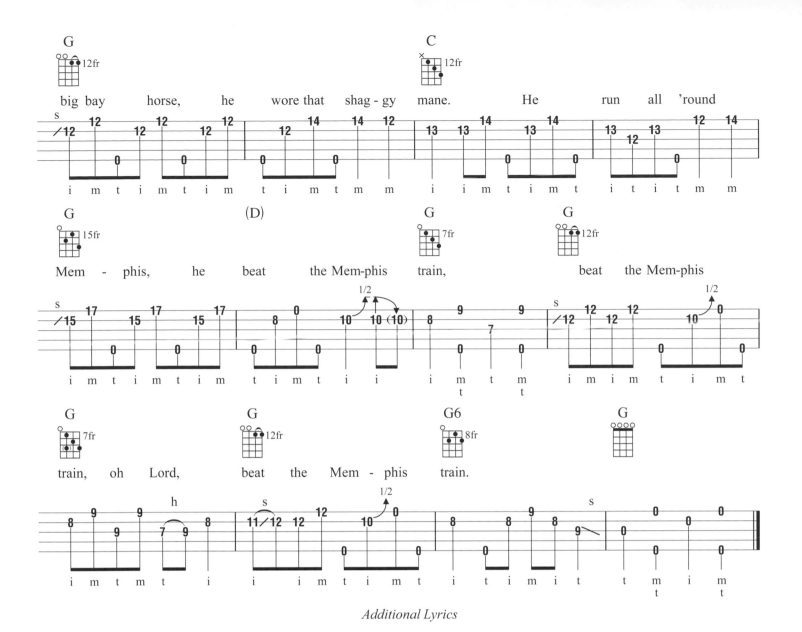

Additional Lyrics

3. Tenbrooks said to Molly, "What makes your head so red?"
   "Running in the hot sun with a fever in my head.
   Fever in my head, oh Lord, fever in my head."

4. Molly said to Tenbrooks, "You're looking mighty squirrel."
   Tenbrooks said to Molly, "I'm leaving this old world.
   Leaving this old world, oh Lord, leaving this old world."

5. Out in California where Molly done as she pleased,
   She come back to old Kentucky, got beat with all ease.
   Beat with all ease, oh Lord, beat with all ease.

6. The women's all a laughing, the children all a crying,
   Men all a hollering, old Tenbrooks a flying.
   Old Tenbrooks a flying, Lord, old Tenbrooks a flying.

7. Kiper, Kiper, you're not riding right.
   Molly's beating old Tenbrooks clear out of sight.
   Clear out of sight, oh Lord, clear out of sight.

8. Kiper, Kiper, Kiper my son,
   Give old Tenbrooks the bridle and let old Tenbrooks run.
   Let old Tenbrooks run, oh Lord, let old Tenbrooks run.

9. Go and catch old Tenbrooks and hitch him in the shade.
   We're gonna bury old Molly in a coffin ready-made.
   In a coffin ready-made, oh Lord, in a coffin ready-made.

Mountain Dew

Words and Music by Scott Wiseman and Bascom Lunsford

In 1928, banjo picker/folklorist/lawyer Bascom Lamar Lunsford wrote this song about illegal, home-made whiskey (moonshine), and in 1935 Scotty Wiseman improved the lyrics. Lunsford was so impressed, he sold the song to Scotty for $25, in order to buy a train ticket home from a folk festival. Wiseman's recording with his wife Lulu Belle became the version performed by countless old-time and country musicians, and bluegrassers, the Stanley Brothers and Flatt and Scruggs have also recorded it. The first-position solo below is what Ralph Stanley played on a Rebel Records Lp called *Ralph Stanley and the Clinch Mountain Boys*. The second up-the-neck solo is the author's Stanley-style arrangement.

G tuning:
(5th-1st) G-D-G-B-D

Key of G

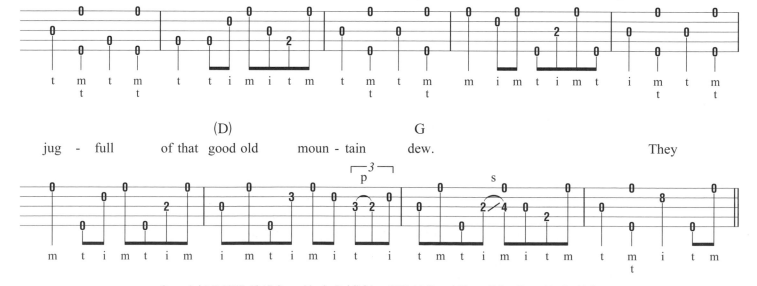

Chorus

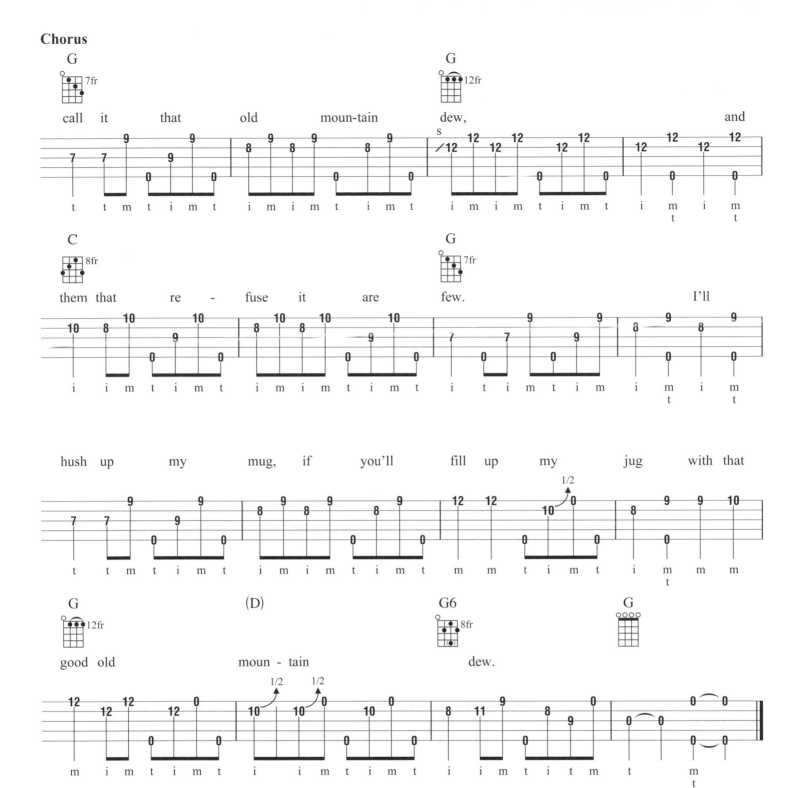

Additional Lyrics

2. Now Mister Roosevelt told 'em just how he felt
   When he heard that the dry law'd gone through.
   If your liquor's too red, it'll swell up your head.
   You better stick to that good ole mountain dew.

3. The preacher rode by with his head hasted high,
   Said his wife had been down with the flu.
   He thought that I ought to sell him a quart
   Of my good ole mountain dew.

4. Well, my uncle Snort, he's sawed off and short,
   He measures four feet two.
   But he feels like a giant when you give him a pint
   Of that good old mountain dew.

My Rose of Old Kentucky

Words and Music by Bill Monroe

Bill Monroe could fill an album or two with songs he wrote that mention his home state, Kentucky. This one dates back to 1947, and it has been covered by a long list of stars in the bluegrass firmament, including the Osborne Brothers, Doyle Lawson and Quicksilver, Del McCoury, J. D. Crowe, the Stanley Brothers, Jimmy Martin and Byron Berline. The arrangement below shows two ways to play the verse: in a low and a high register.

G tuning:
(5th-1st) G-D-G-B-D

Key of G

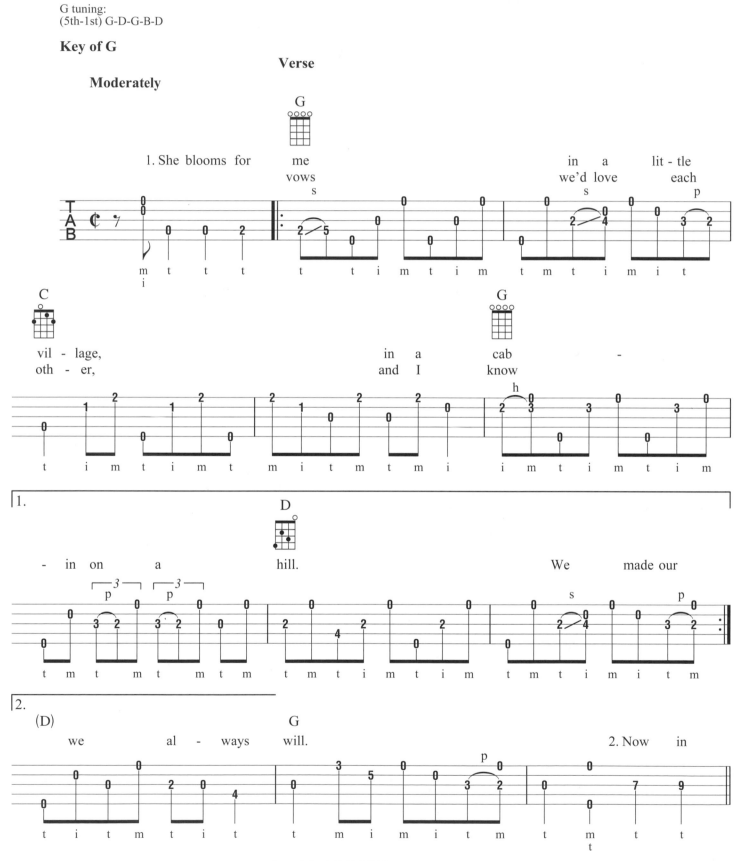

Verse

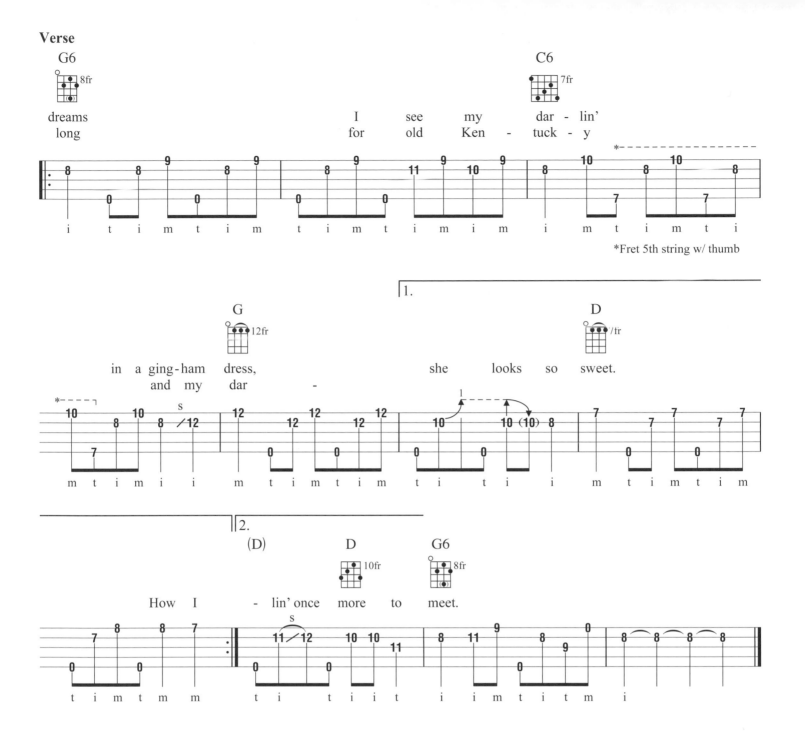

Additional Lyrics

Chorus: She's my rose of old Kentucky.
I've watched her bloom as the years go by,
And to me there'll never be another.
I'll love her 'til the day I die.

3. Now I know you've often wondered,
So I'll tell you the reason why
She's my rose of old Kentucky,
I'll love her 'til the day I die.

Nine Pound Hammer

Traditional African-American

This work song was recorded by string bands in the 1920s and by the Monroe Brothers in the 1930s. Bill Monroe continued to record and perform it later with his Bluegrass Boys, and Merle Travis's 1947 fingerpicking guitar version also helped popularize the tune.

G tuning:
(5th-1st) G-D-G-B-D

Key of G

Moderately

Verse

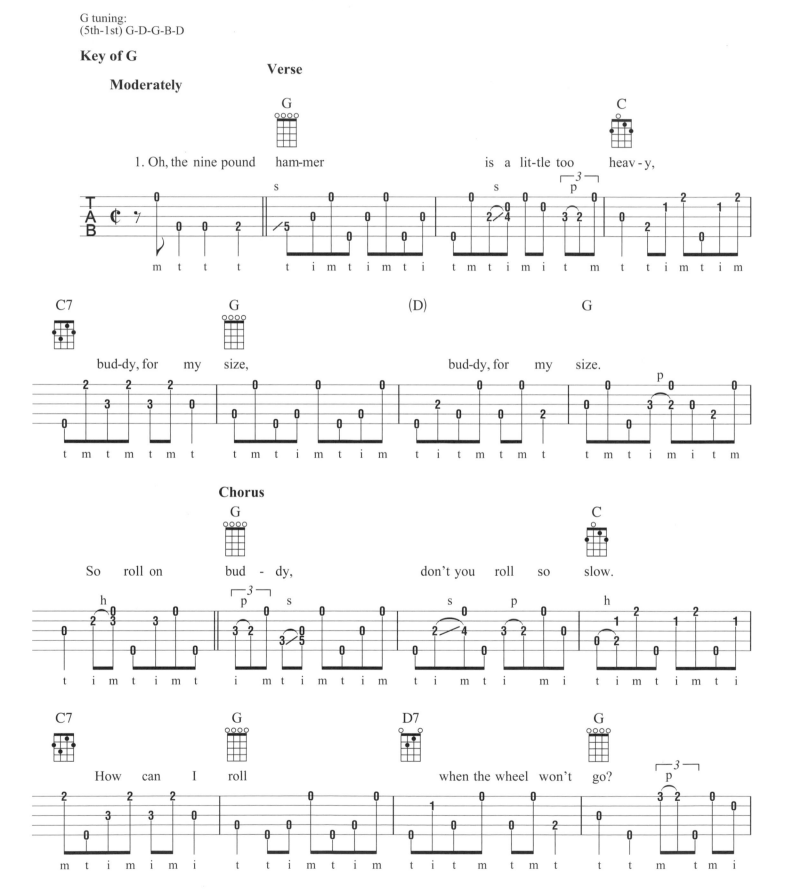

Chorus

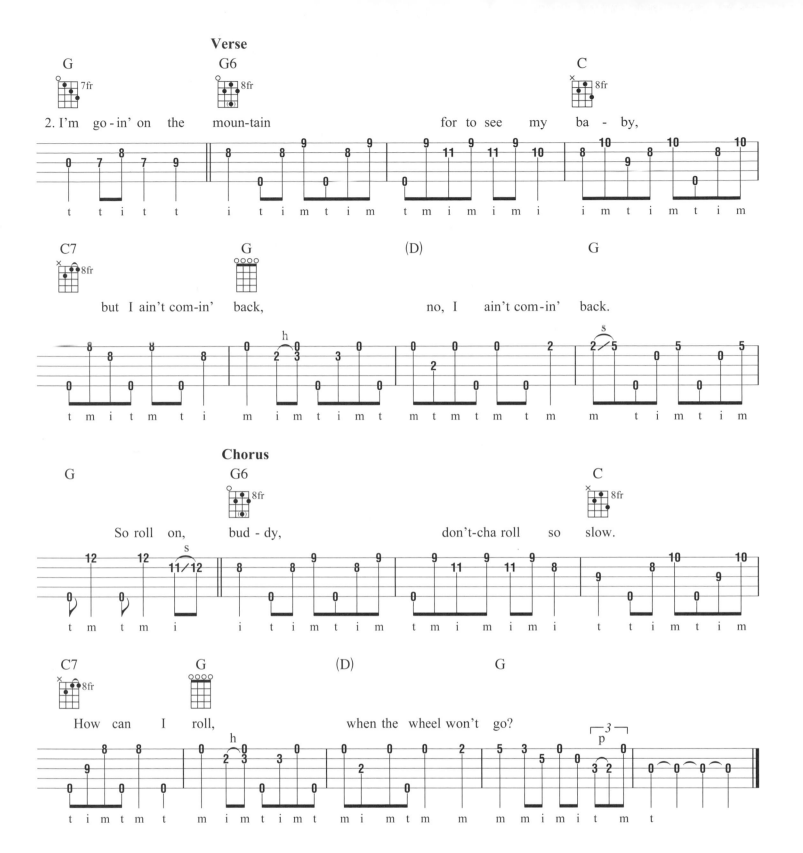

Additional Lyrics

3. There ain't one hammer in this tunnel
   That'll ring like mine, that'll ring like mine.

4. Rings like silver, and it shines like gold.
   Rings like silver, and it shines like gold.

5. Oh, the nine pound hammer, that killed John Henry
   Ain't a gonna kill me, it ain't gonna kill me.

Rawhide

By Bill Monroe

Bill Monroe's instrumental, "Rawhide," has been called "the Mount Everest" of bluegrass instrumentals, because of its speed and many chord changes. He named it after an actor friend of his who was featured in many cowboy movies, including the 1951 western film, *Rawhide*. The banjo solo below was on Monroe's early 1950s recording of the tune; it's probably the lightning-fast picking of Bluegrass Boy, Rudy Lyle. (It can be found on an Lp called *Bill Monroe Anthology*.) The tune is always played in the key of C, and most banjo players (including Lyle) capo at the 5th fret and tune the fifth string to C.

G tuning:
(5th-1st) G-D-G-B-D

Key of G

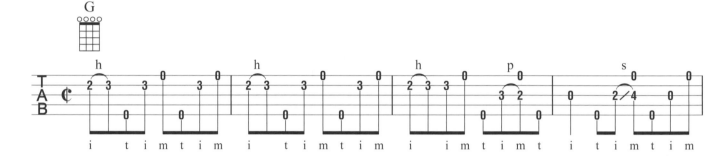

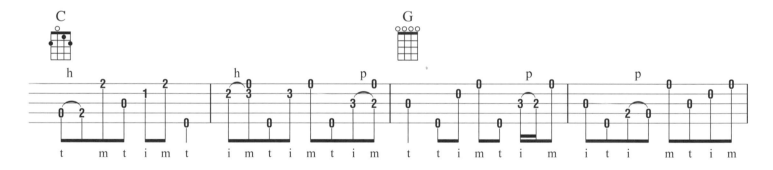

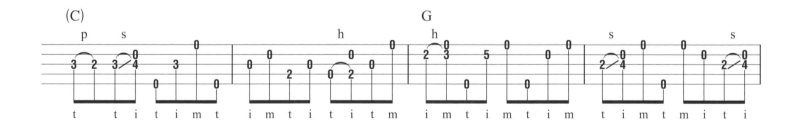

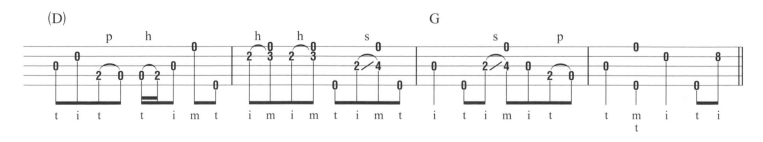

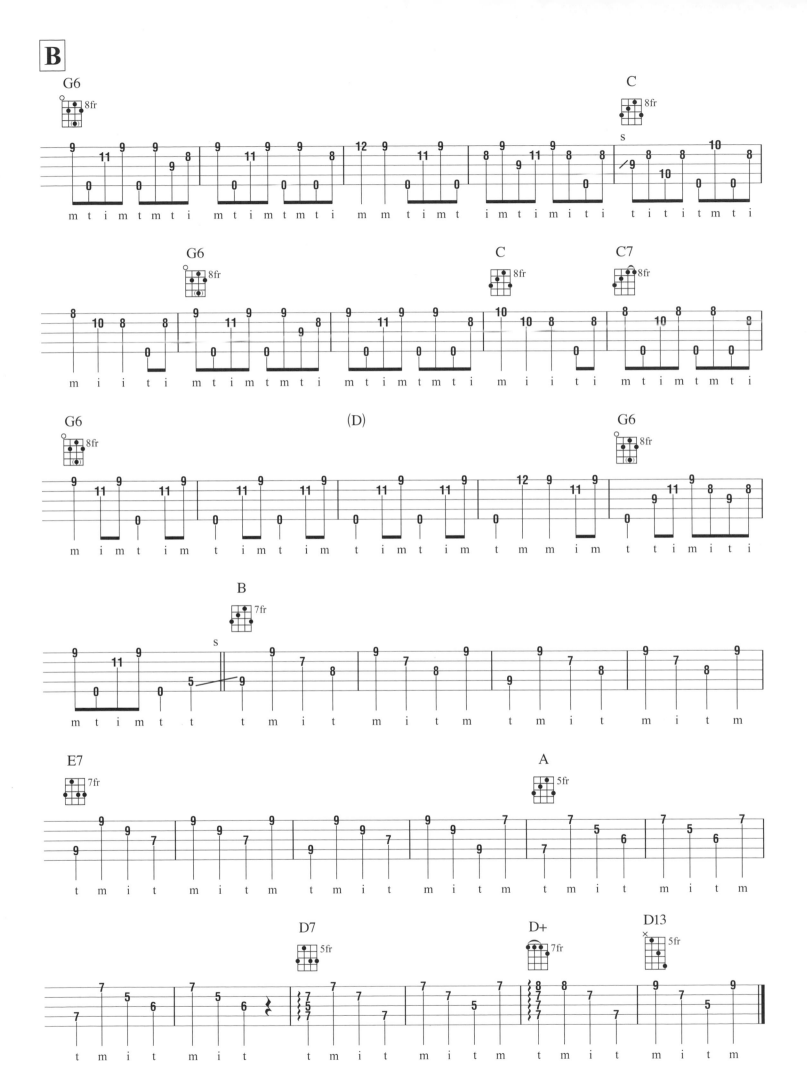

Rocky Top

Words and Music by Boudleaux Bryant and Felice Bryant

Felice and Boudleaux Bryant were the songwriting couple responsible for many Everly Brothers hits ("All I Have to Do Is Dream," "Bye Bye Love," etc.) as well as "Love Hurts" (a hit for Roy Orbison), "Raining in My Heart" (Buddy Holly), "You're the Reason God Made Oklahoma" and many more. They wrote "Rocky Top" in 1967, and the Osborne Brothers' rendition became one of the few bluegrass recordings to reach the country charts; Lynn Anderson's cover charted again in 1970. Sonny Osborne's solos on the 1967 recording are transcribed below, except for the first half of the chorus; Bobby Osborne played a mandolin break in that spot, so the author has substituted a banjo solo there. The Osbornes played the song in B, and Sonny was capoed at the 4th fret with his fifth string tuned to B.

G tuning:
(5th-1st) G-D-G-B-D

Key of G

Verse
Moderately

G   Cadd9   G

1. Wish that I was on old Rock - y Top,

(Em)   D   G

down in the Ten - nes - see hills.

   C   G

Ain't no smog - gy smoke on Rock - y Top,

(Em)   D   G

ain't no tel - e - phone bills.

Chorus

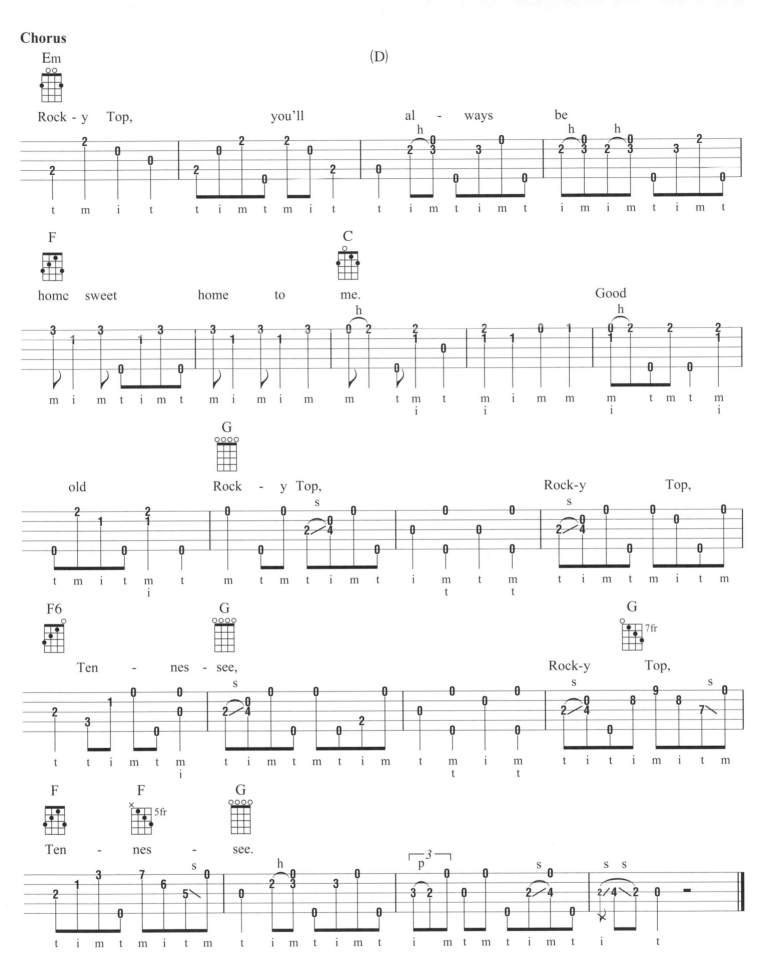

Additional Lyrics

2. Once two strangers climbed old Rocky Top,
   Looking for a moonshine still.
   Strangers ain't come down from Rocky Top.
   Reckon they never will.

3. Corn won't grow at all on Rocky Top,
   Dirt's too rocky by far.
   That's why all the folks on Rocky Top
   Get their corn from a jar.

Roll in My Sweet Baby's Arms

Traditional

Posey Rorer, Buster Carter and Preston Young recorded a version of this old folk song in 1931, and Flatt and Scruggs' 1951 arrangement has been covered by countless bluegrass and country artists. The verse and chorus are musically identical.

G tuning:
(5th-1st) G-D-G-B-D

Key of G

Verse

Fast

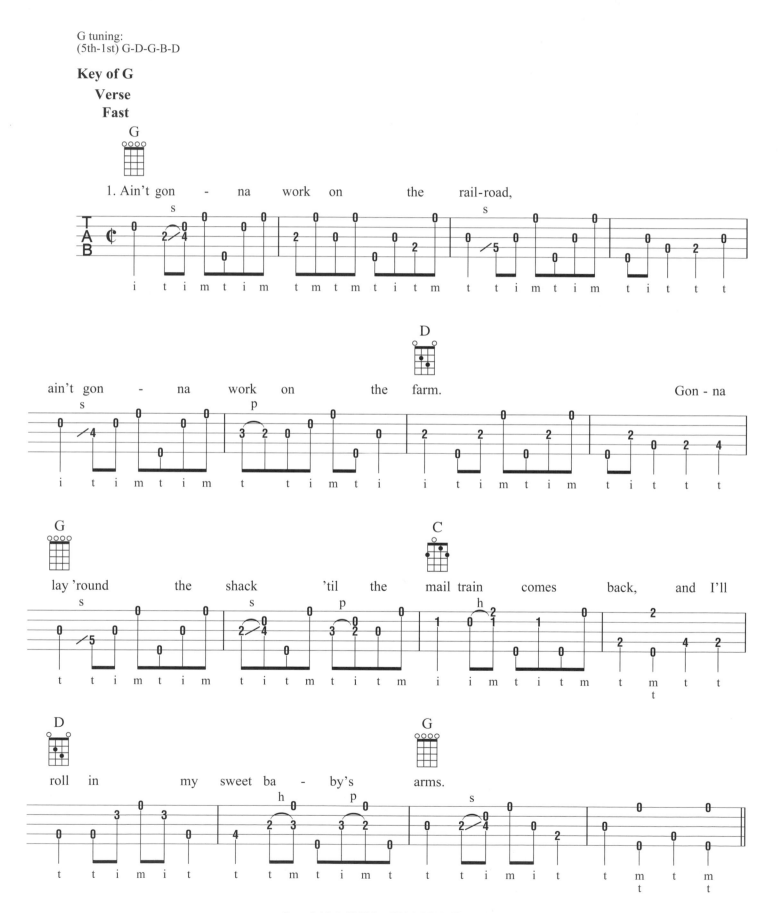

Chorus

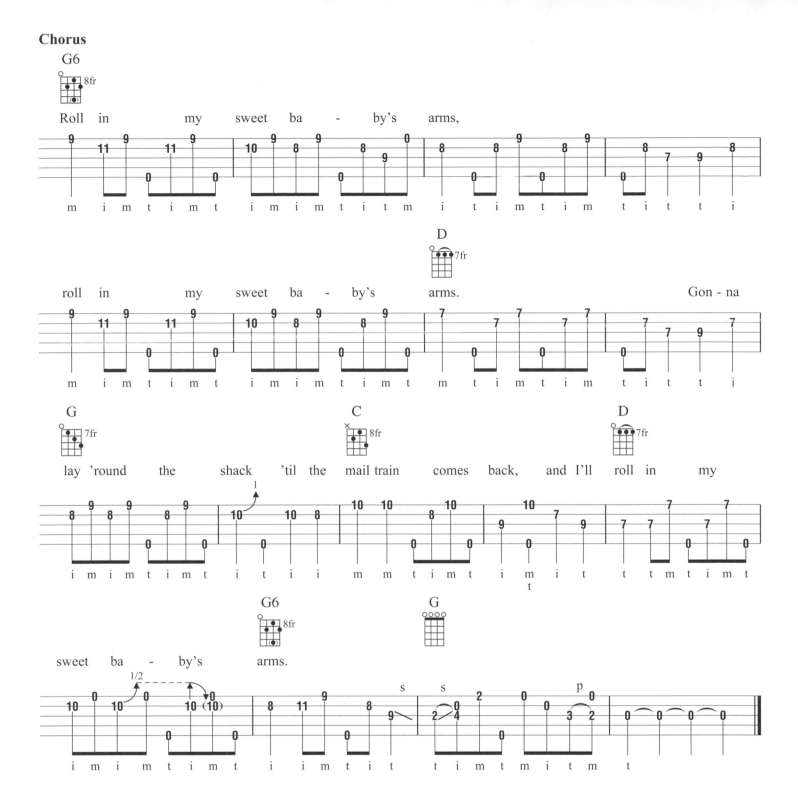

Additional Lyrics

2. Now, where was you last Friday night
   While I was lyin' in jail?
   Walkin' the streets with another man,
   You wouldn't even go my bail.

3. I know your parents don't like me;
   They drove me away from your door.
   If I had my life to live over again,
   I'd never go there anymore.

4. Mama's a beauty operator,
   Sister can weave and can spin.
   Dad's got an interest in the old cotton mill,
   Just watch the money roll in.

Salt Creek

By Bill Monroe and Bradford Keith

In 1929, old-time fiddler Clark Kessinger recorded "Salt River," a fiddle tune named after a river in Kentucky. In 1964, when banjo player Bill Keith was in Bill Monroe's band, the two Bills re-worked the tune and recorded it with the name "Salt Creek," which is the creek in Indiana where Monroe held the annual bluegrass "Bean Blossom" festival. Both Bills are gone now, but the festival continues, and the fiddle tune is still played by bluegrass bands. Bill Keith's first time around the tune is transcribed below. The tune is played in the key of A, with the usual capo and fifth string settings.

G tuning:
(5th-1st) G-D-G-B-D

Key of G

Salty Dog Blues

Words and Music by Wiley A. Morris and Zeke Morris

There are bluesy recordings of "Salty Dog Blues" as early as the 1920s (Papa Charlie Jackson, Clara Smith and others), but the 1945 Morris Brothers' version was the model for Flatt and Scruggs' 1950 recording, and their arrangement is covered by countless bluegrass bands. (Earl Scruggs played with the Morris Brothers when he was fifteen years old, many years before his stint with Bill Monroe and later collaboration with Lester Flatt.) The solo below is transcribed from Flatt and Scruggs' 1950 recording. The band tuned their instruments up a half step, so the recording is in G#.

G tuning:
(5th-1st) G-D-G-B-D

Key of G

Fast

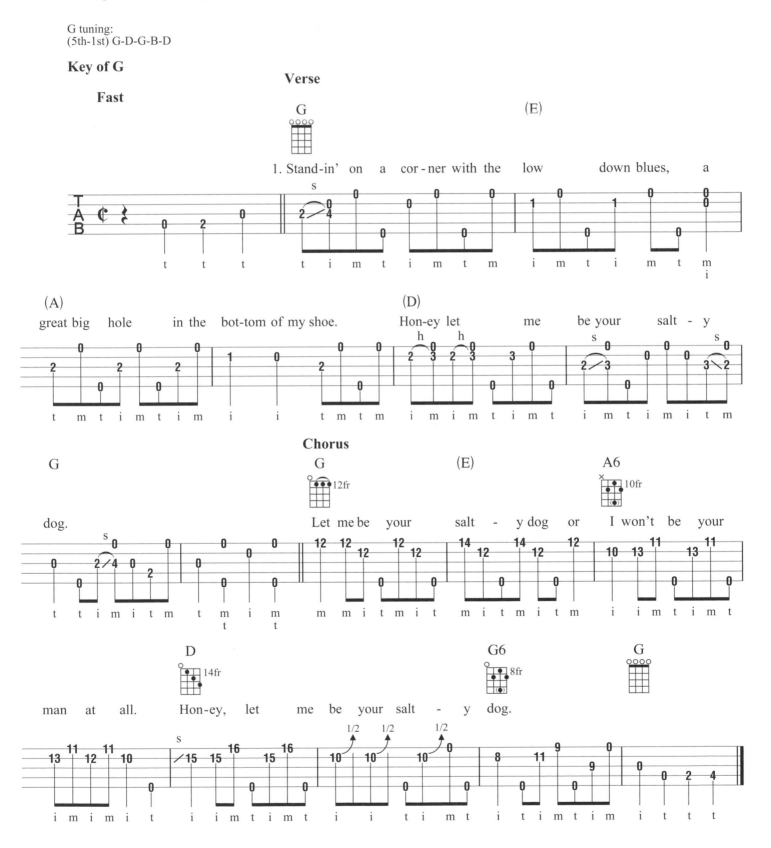

Soldier's Joy

Traditional

One of the oldest and most popular fiddle tunes, "Soldier's Joy" comes from Scotland, where it has been played for over two hundred years. There is sheet music on it dating back to the eighteenth century. It is usually performed as an instrumental, but the lyrics that are sometimes sung indicate that the "joy" in question is morphine…or payday (either of which could make a soldier happy).

The first arrangement below shows one way to play in the key of D: the fifth string is tuned up to A and no capo is used. The second time around the tune, the fifth string is still in A, but the banjo is capoed up two frets. This version is a good example of melodic picking. The chord grids are not really *chords*, they are fingering positions that allow you to play those scalar, melodic licks.

Tuning:
(5th-1st) A-D-G-B-D

Key of D

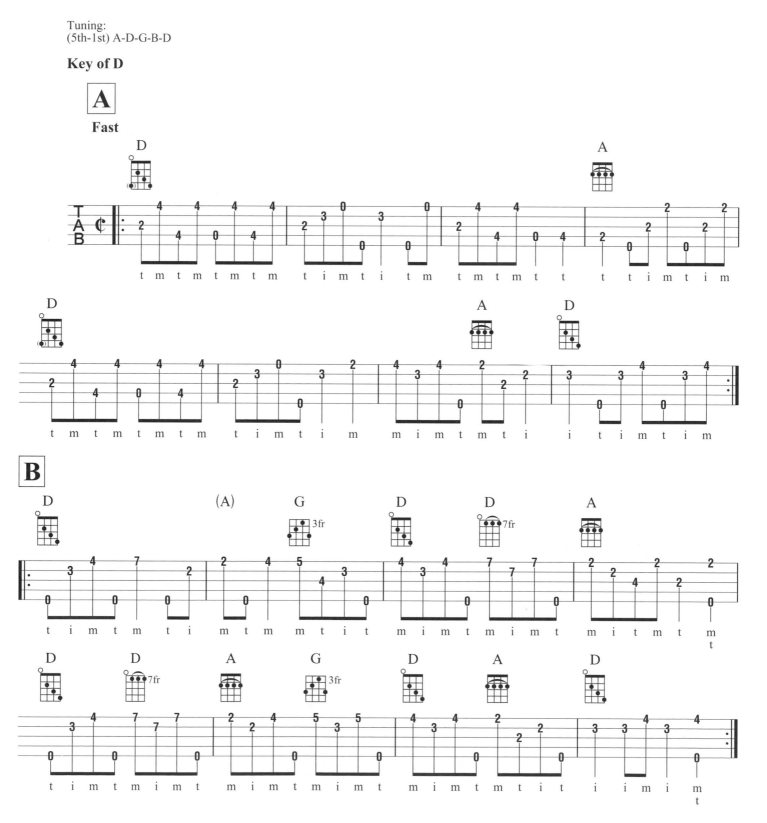

Tuning, capo II:
(5th-1st) A-D-G-B-D

Key of C (Sounds in D)

A

Fast

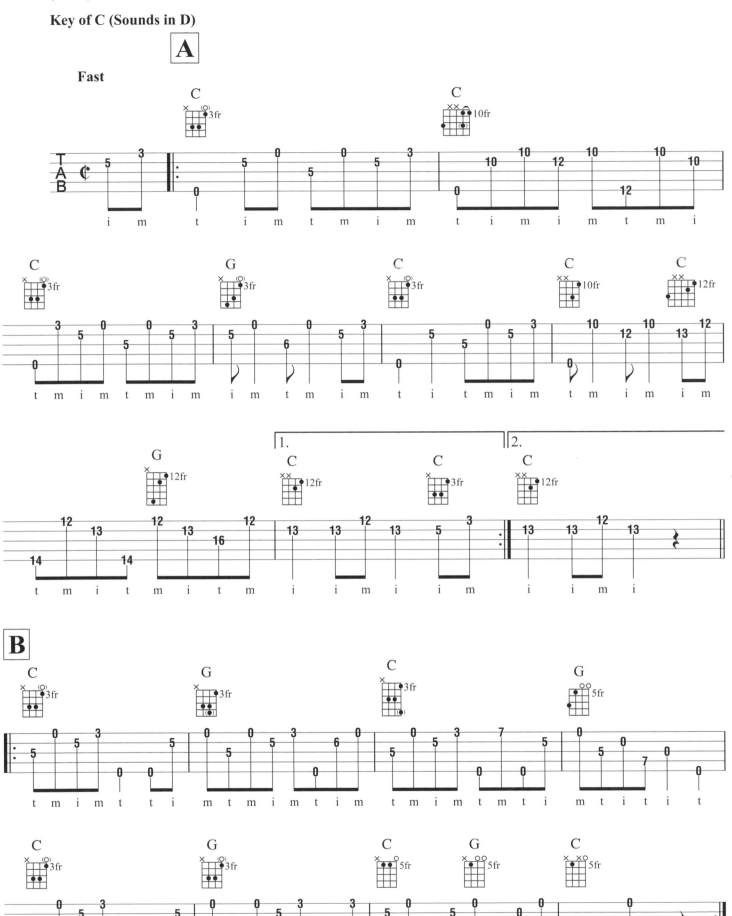

Think of What You've Done

Words and Music by Carter Stanley

This classic Stanley Brothers tune, written by Carter Stanley, has been recorded by Larry Sparks, Ricky Skaggs, Hot Rize, Molly Tuttle, and many others. The first solo, below, is what Ralph Stanley played on the original 1958 recording of the tune. Typically, Ralph Stanley leads almost exclusively with his index finger, playing primarily forward rolls. The second solo shows how he might have played an up-the-neck solo. (The recording sounds like the key of C♯; it's probably in C with the band tuned a bit high. Ralph capoed at the 5th fret and tuned the fifth string to C.)

G tuning:
(5th-1st) G-D-G-B-D

Key of G

Verse

Fast

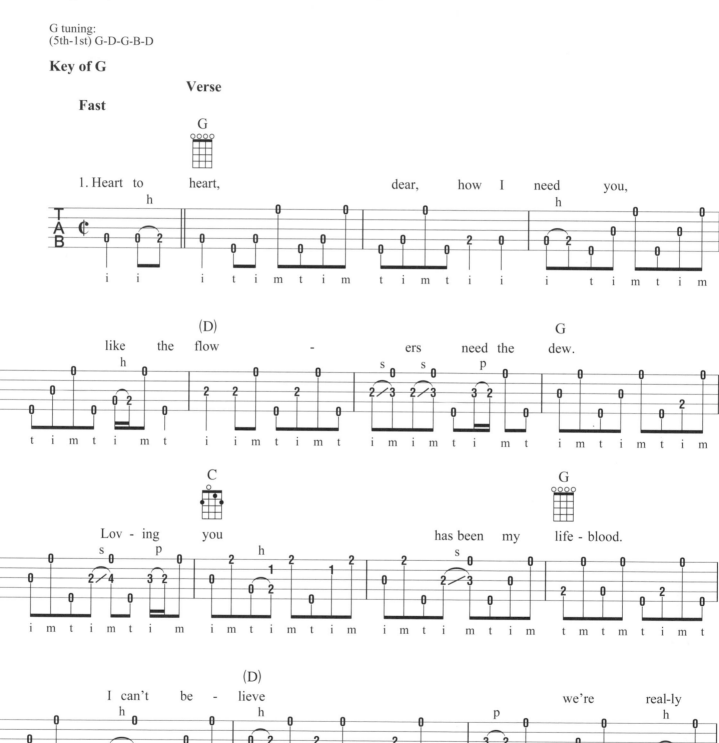

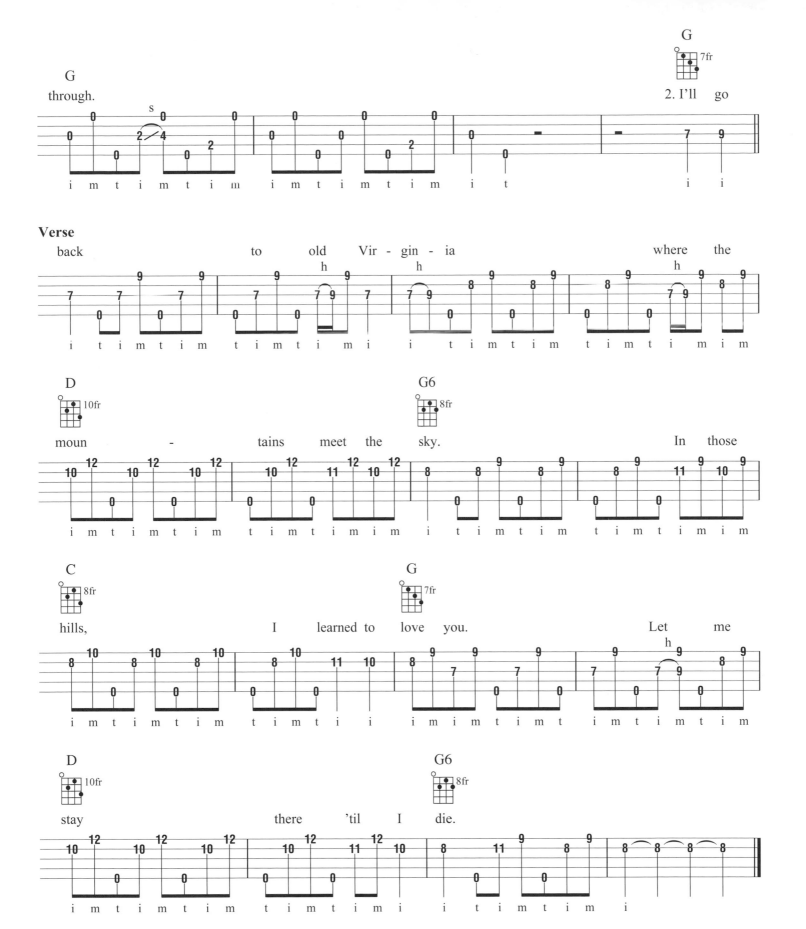

Additional Lyrics

Chorus: Is it true that I have lost you?
Am I not the only one?
After all this pain and sorrow, darlin',
Think of what you've done.

Uncle Pen

Words and Music by Bill Monroe

Bill Monroe called his fiddle-playing uncle, Pendleton Vandiver, "the fellow that I learned how to play from."
Uncle Pen taught him about keeping time and offered playing tips. When a very young Monroe accompanied
Pen at square dances and performances, he learned some repertoire that stayed with him throughout his career.
Monroe wrote the song about his uncle around 1950, and it has become a bluegrass standard. Usually, the
banjo only plays a chorus, if it is featured at all, but a verse and chorus are in the arrangement below, in both
high and low registers. The song is always played in the key of A.

G tuning:
(5th-1st) G-D-G-B-D

Key of G

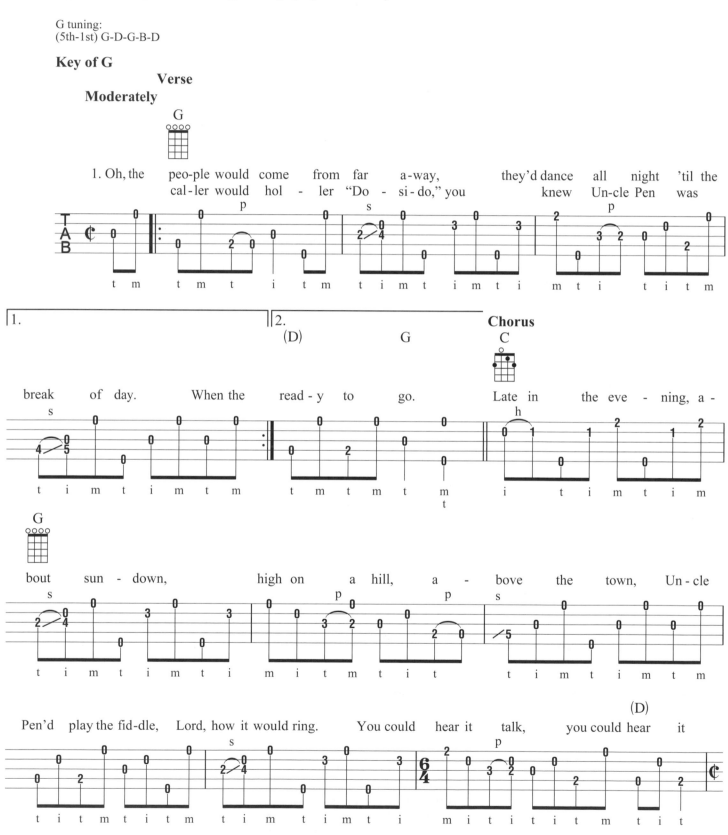

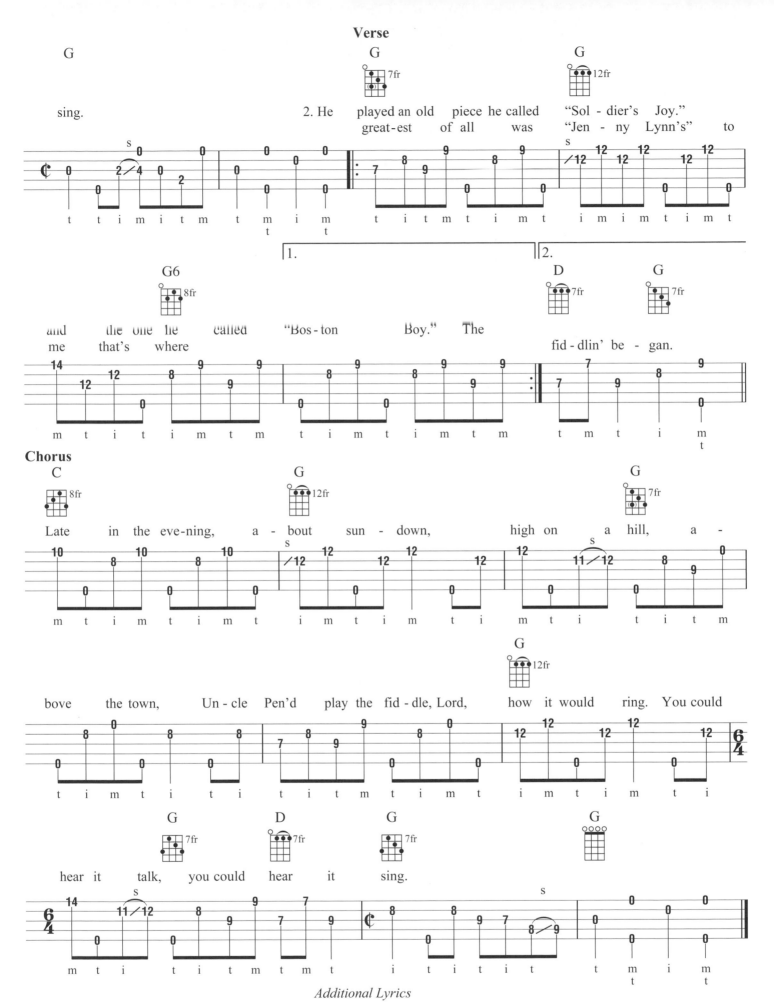

Additional Lyrics

3. I'll never forget that mournful day
   When Uncle Pen was called away.
   They hung up his fiddle, they hung up his bow,
   They knew it was time for him to go.

Wabash Cannonball

Words and Music by A.P. Carter

No one seems to know who Daddy Cleaton was (or Daddy Claxton, as he is called in most versions of the song). Many say the Wabash Cannonball was a mythical train, but the lyric and tune come from a late 1800s song called "The Great Rock Island Route," about an actual train route that stretched across many states. In 1929, the Carter Family recorded a version of the song that had been re-written as "The Wabash Cannonball" in 1904. Opry star, Roy Acuff recorded the Carter Family version in 1936, and it became his signature song. The words vary from one performer to another, but the lyrics here belong to the Carter Family.

There are two banjo solos below, one in the key of G, one in C.

G tuning:
(5th-1st) G-D-G-B-D

Key of G

Moderately

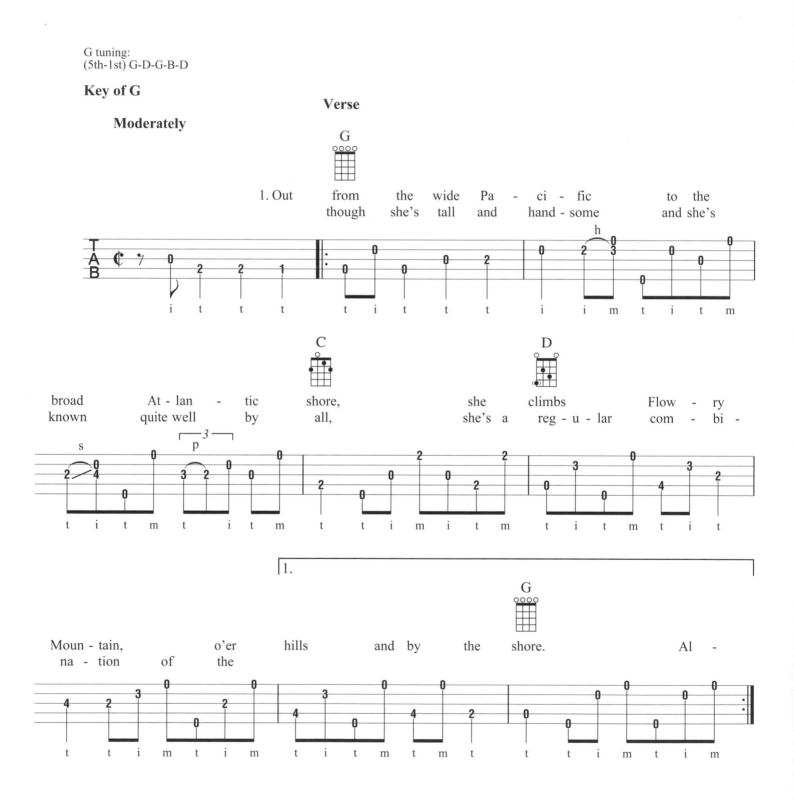

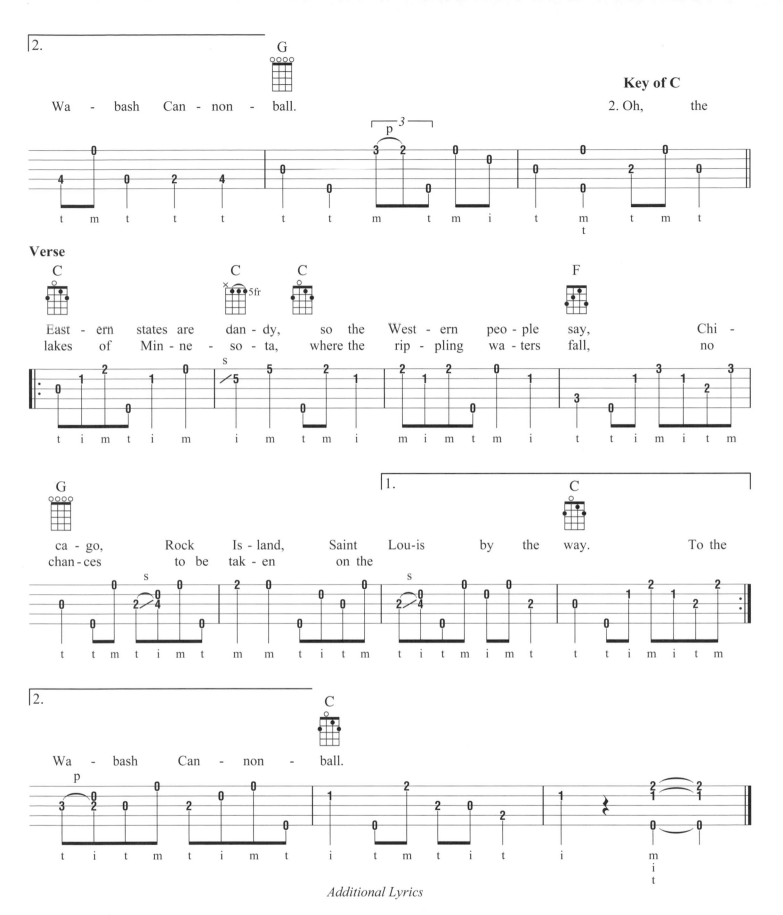

Additional Lyrics

3. Oh, listen to the jingle, the rumor and the roar
   As she glides along the woodland, o'er hills and by the shore.
   She climbs the Flow'ry Mountain, hear the merry hobo squall,
   She glides along the woodland, the Wabash Cannonball.

4. Oh, here's old Daddy Cleaton, let his name forever be,
   And long be remembered in the courts of Tennessee.
   For he is a good ol' rounder 'til the curtain around him fall,
   He'll be carried back to victory on the Wabash Cannonball.

Wagon Wheel

Words and Music by Bob Dylan and Ketch Secor

Bob Dylan wrote the chorus ("Rock me mama…") for the 1973 film *Pat Garrett and Billy the Kid*, and twenty-five years later, Ketch Secor wrote the verses. In 2004, the song became a huge hit for Secor's group, Old Crow Medicine Show; and in 2013 it was a #1 hit for Darius Rucker. The song has become a campfire classic and a "Free Bird-level" request of bands all over the world.

G tuning:
(5th-1st) G-D-G-B-D

Key of G

   Verse

    Moderately slow

Chorus

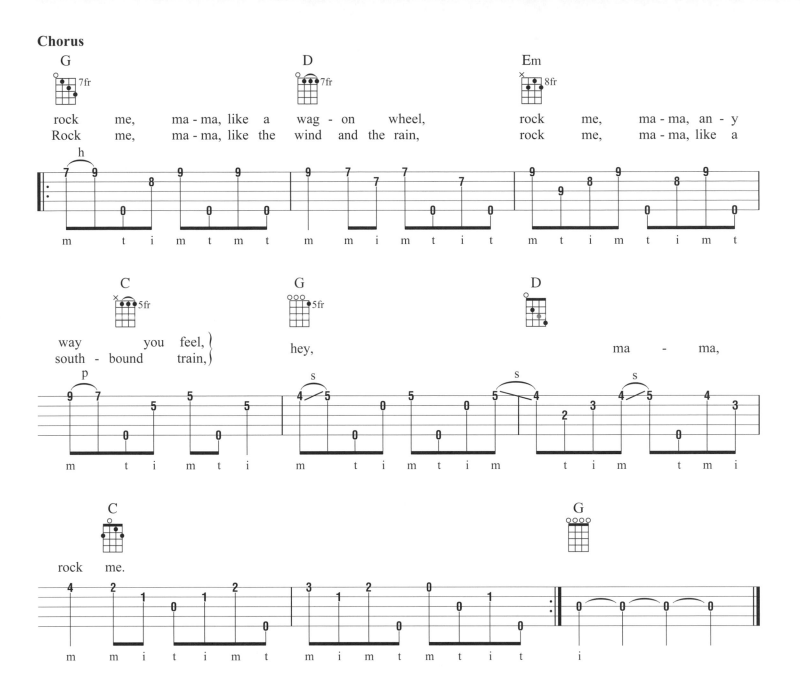

Additional Lyrics

2. Runnin' from the cold up in New England,
   I was born to be a fiddler in an old-time string band.
   My baby plays the guitar, I pick a banjo now.
   Oh, the North Country winters keep a getting' me now.
   Lost my money playin' poker, so I had to up and leave,
   But I ain't a turnin' back to livin' that old life no more.

3. Walkin' to the south out of Roanoke,
   I caught a trucker out of Philly, had a nice long toke.
   But he's a headed west from the Cumberland Gap to Johnson City, Tennessee.
   And I gotta get a move on before the sun.
   I hear my baby callin' my name and I know that she's the only one,
   And if I die in Raleigh, at least I will die free.

Way Downtown

Traditional
Arranged by Doc Watson

An old string band standard that borrows verses from many other folk songs, "Way Downtown" was popularized in the early 1960s by Doc Watson, whose brilliant solo guitar performance inspired bluegrass bands to take up the song. It's safe to say that Doc and Clarence White are responsible for transforming the bluegrass guitarist's role from that of accompanist to "accompanist-who-also-solos."

The banjo solos below are good examples of playing in the key of D, Scruggs style, without a capo. Be sure to tune your 5th string up to A.

Tuning:
(5th-1st) A-D-G-B-D

Key of D

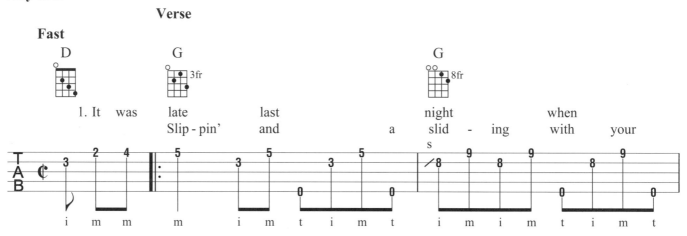

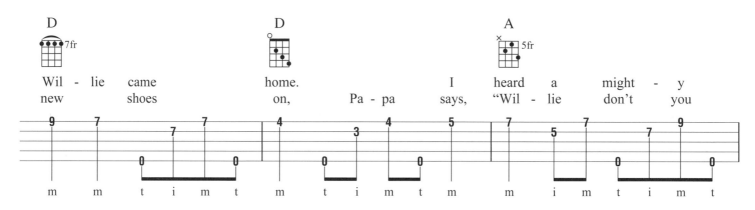

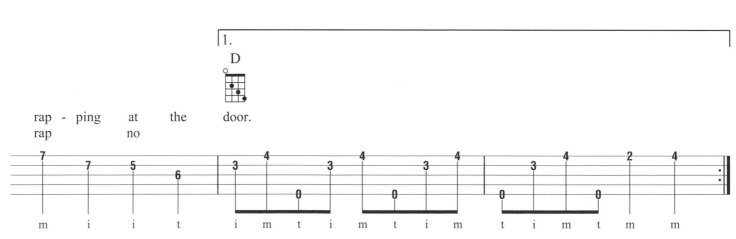

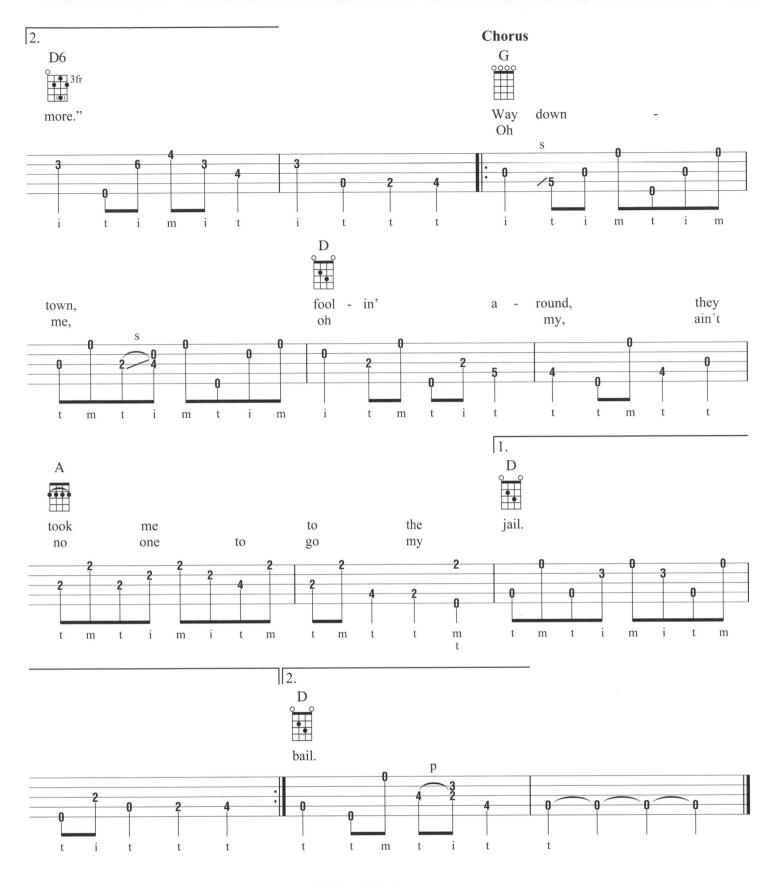

Additional Lyrics

2. One old shirt is all I have
   And a dollar is all I crave.
   Ain't brought nothing into this world
   And I ain't gonna take nothing to my grave.

3. Wish I was down at my old Sally's house,
   Sittin' in her big armchair,
   One arm around my old guitar
   And the other one around my dear.

4. Where were you last Friday night,
   While I was locked up in jail?
   You were walking the streets with some other man,
   Wouldn't even go my bail.

Wayfaring Stranger

Southern American Folk Hymn

This gospel favorite goes back to the early 1800s, possibly earlier. It was sung at Appalachian revival services and spread west with the pioneers. Folksinger Burl Ives popularized it in the 1940s, followed by Joan Baez in the '60s, Emmylou Harris in the '80s, and Johnny Cash in 2000. Bill Monroe recorded and performed many versions of it from the 1950s, until his last years. More recently, Ed Sheeran's cover has been widely viewed on YouTube. The arrangement below is a good example of a bluegrass style solo in a minor key. This one also has the 5th string tuned to A.

Tuning:
(5th-1st) A-D-G-B-D

Key of A minor

Moderately slow

Chorus

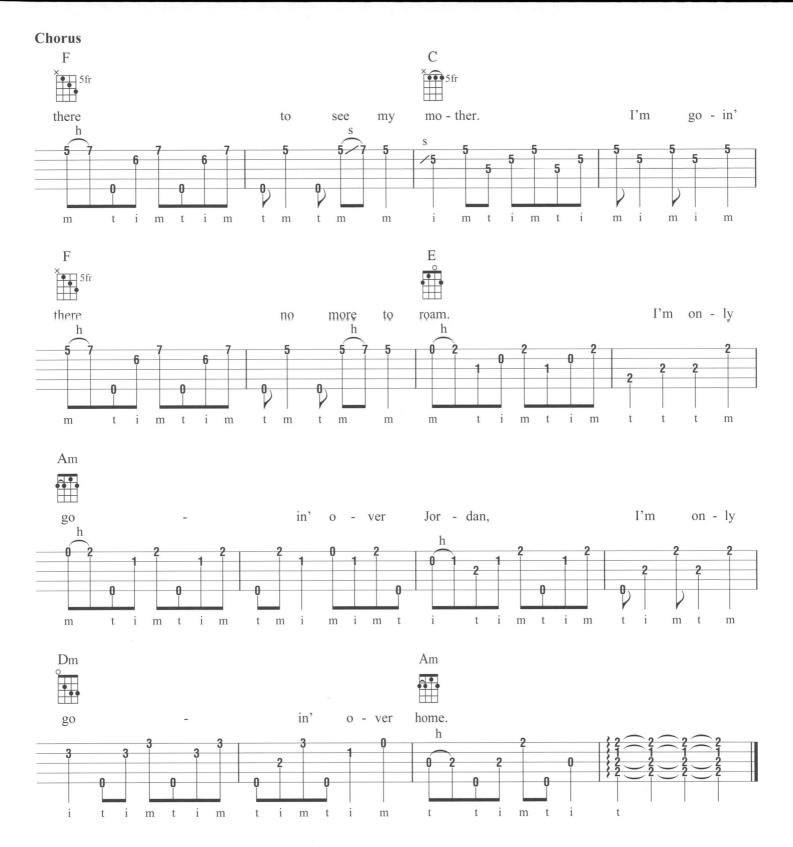

Additional Lyrics

2. I know dark clouds will gather 'round me;
   I know my way is rough and steep.
   But beautiful fields lie just beyond me
   Where souls redeemed their vigil keep.

Chorus: I'm going there to meet my mother,
   She said she'd meet me when I come.
   I'm just a going over Jordan,
   I'm only going over home.

White Dove

Words and Music by Carter Stanley

In 1949, in the back seat of a car heading home, his brother Ralph at the wheel, Carter Stanley wrote this beautiful meditation on the loss of his parents. The plaintive waltz has become a favorite among bluegrass performers. The chorus is only slightly different from the verses. Like "In the Pines," the solo below is a good example of playing in waltz (3/4) time, bluegrass style. The Stanley Brothers played the song in the key of F. You could match that by capoing at the 5th fret and tuning the fifth string up to C. The second time around the tune is a good example of playing in the key of F without a capo, with the 5th string tuned up to A.

G tuning:
(5th-1st) G-D-G-B-D

Key of C

Slow

Verse

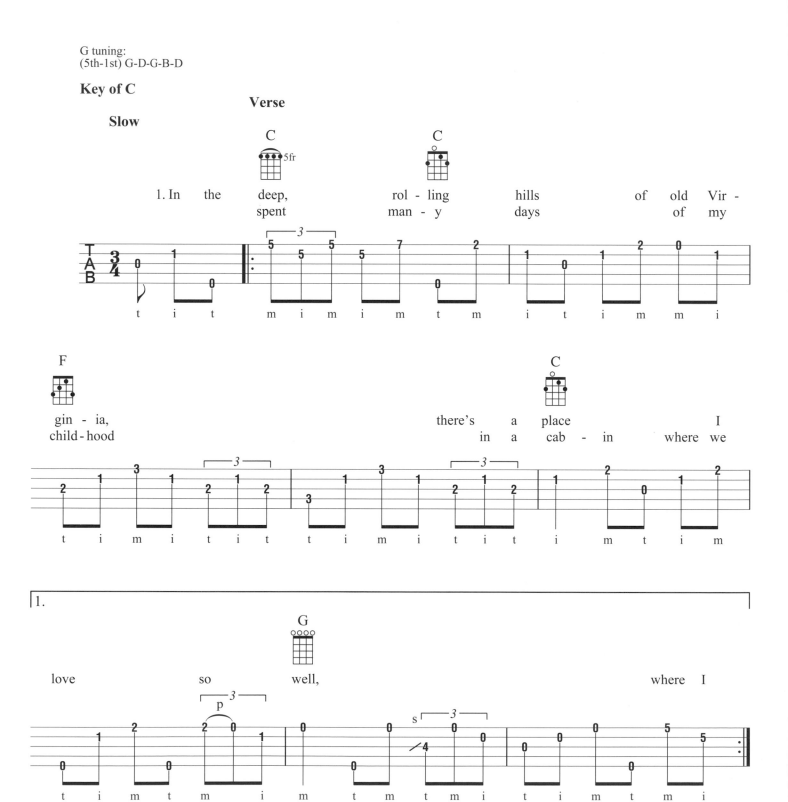

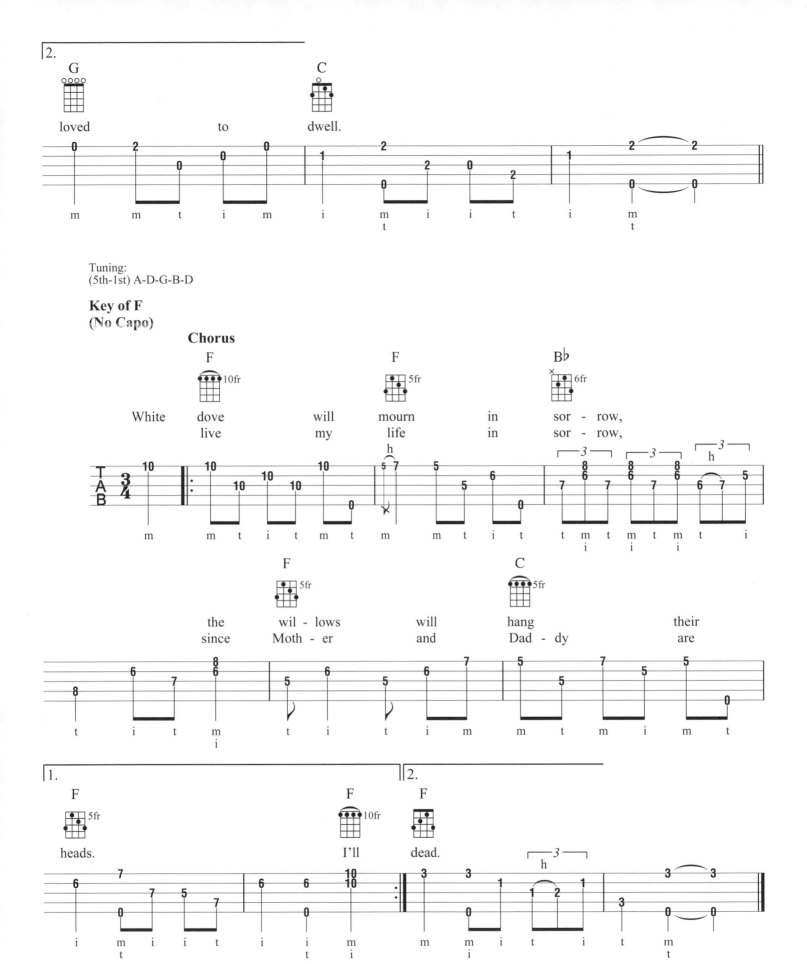

Additional Lyrics

2. We were all so happy there together
   In our peaceful little mountain home,
   But the Savior needs angels up in heaven.
   Now they sing around that great white throne.

3. As the years roll by, I often wonder
   If we will all be together someday.
   And each night as I wander through the graveyard,
   Darkness finds me as I kneel to pray.

Will the Circle Be Unbroken

Words by Ada R. Habershon
Music by Charles H. Gabriel

In 1935, the Carter Family recorded "Can the Circle Be Unbroken," a revised version of a 1907 hymn ("Will the Circle Be Unbroken") in which the singer describes his or her mother's funeral and declares that we'll all be reunited in heaven. The Carter family arrangement has become extremely popular and is often sung as a finale to a country music or bluegrass concert. Numerous singers and bands have recorded the tune.

G tuning:
(5th-1st) G-D-G-B-D

Key of G

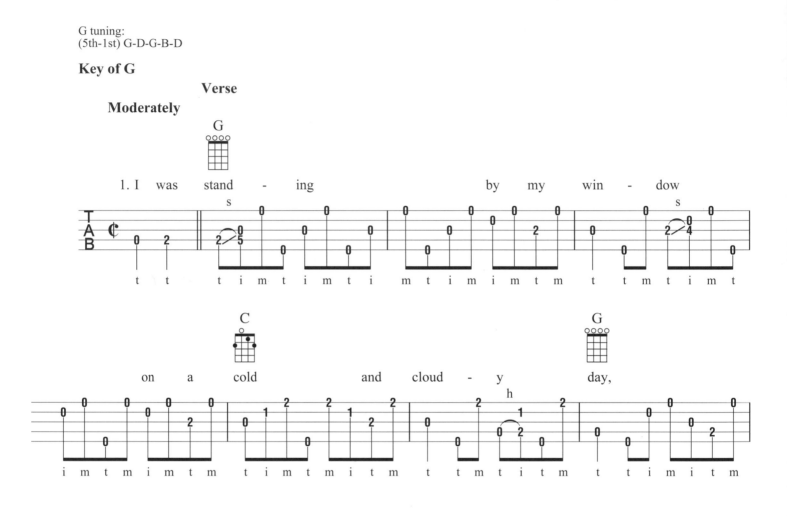

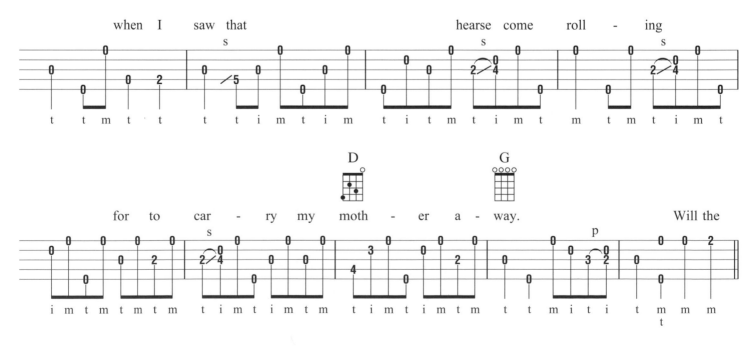

Chorus

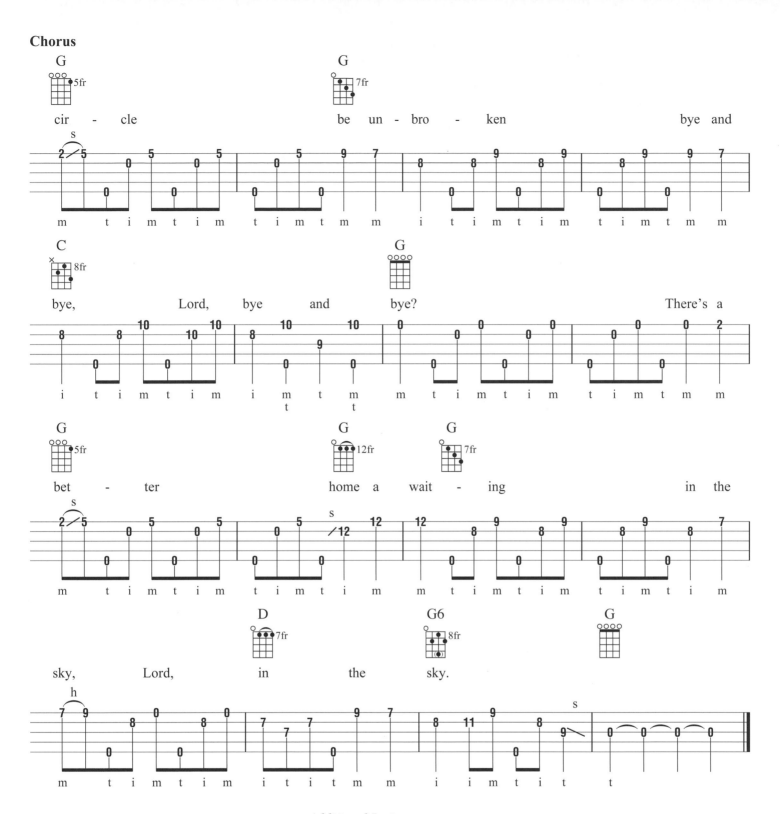

Additional Lyrics

2. Lord, I told the undertaker,
   "Undertaker, please drive slow,
   For this body you are hauling,
   Lord, I hate to see her go."

3. I followed close behind her,
   Tried to hold up and be brave.
   But I could not hide my sorrow
   When they laid her in the grave.

4. Went back home, Lord, my home was lonesome,
   Since my mother, she was gone.
   All my brothers, sisters cryin',
   What a home so sad and 'lone.

Wreck of the Old 97

Traditional

This song accurately describes an actual train wreck that took place in 1903; you can find a photo of the wreckage online. The identity of the composer is in dispute, but Henry Whitter and G.B. Grayson first recorded it in 1923, and the following year, country singer Vernon Dalhart scored the first million-selling country hit with his rendition. The tune has become so popular in the bluegrass and country music worlds that an alternative country band took the name *Old 97's*.

G tuning:
(5th-1st) G-D-G-B-D

Key of G

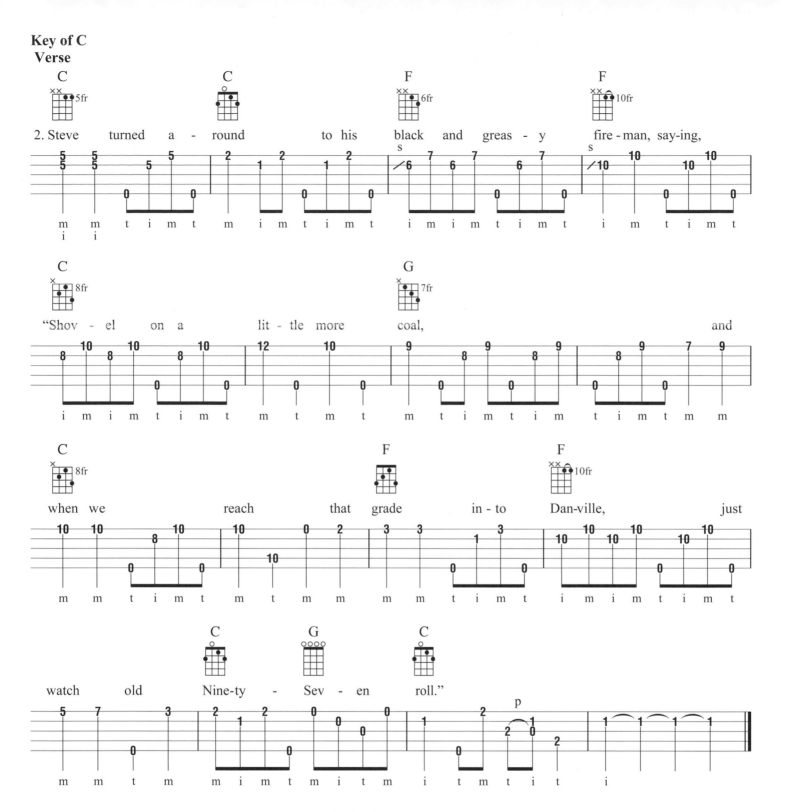

Additional Lyrics

3. It's a long, hard road from Lynchburg to Danville
   And it's lined with a three-mile grade.
   It was on that road that he lost his airbrakes,
   You see what a jump he made.

4. They were going down the track, ninety miles an hour,
   When his whistle broke into a scream.
   He was found in the wreck with his hand on the throttle,
   Scalded to death by the steam.

5. Now all you women, please take warning
   From this day on and learn,
   Never speak harsh words to your kind and loving husband,
   He may leave you and never return.

You Don't Know My Mind

Words and Music by Jimmie Skinner

One of the great tenor singers from the "golden age of bluegrass" (the 1950s), Jimmy Martin spent several years playing guitar and singing in Bill Monroe's Bluegrass Boys before leading his own band, the Sunny Mountain Boys. He helped define the "high lonesome sound" of bluegrass vocals, and wrote several popular bluegrass standards, among them, "You Don't Know My Mind." The song may well be autobiographical, as Martin was a colorful and cantankerous character. The solo below is a transcription of J. D. Crowe's excellent solo on Martin's first recording of "You Don't Know My Mind." Crowe was a Sunny Mountain Boy and went on to form his own band, the New South, whose repertoire pushed the bluegrass envelope and whose various lineups featured now-famous players like Tony Rice and Doyle Lawson.

The band played this song in B♭, so if you want to match the recording, capo at the 3rd fret and tune the fifth string up to B♭. Crowe's solo came after the second chorus. The up-the-neck solo is the author's arrangement.

G tuning:
(5th-1st) G-D-G-B-D

Key of G

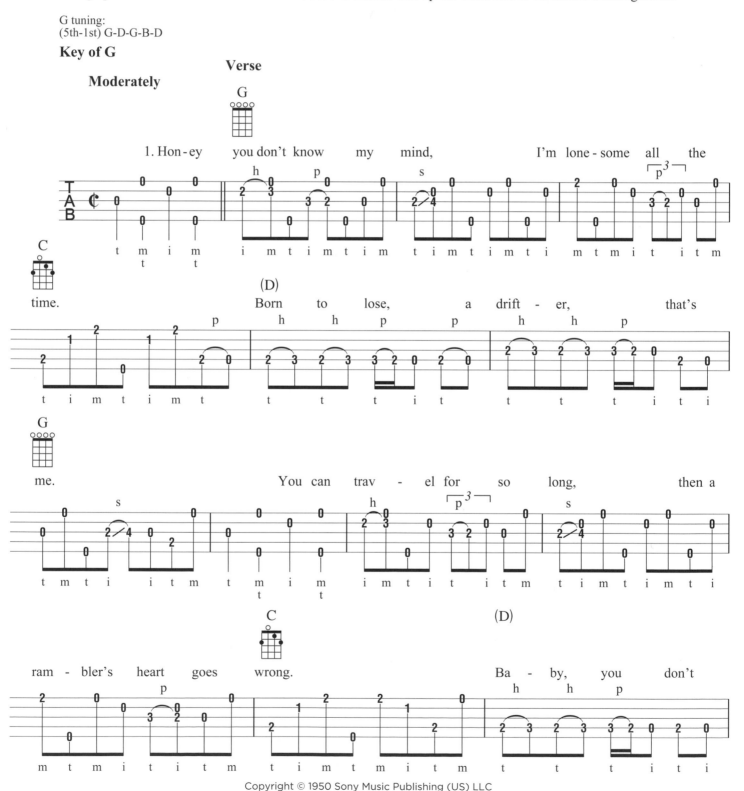

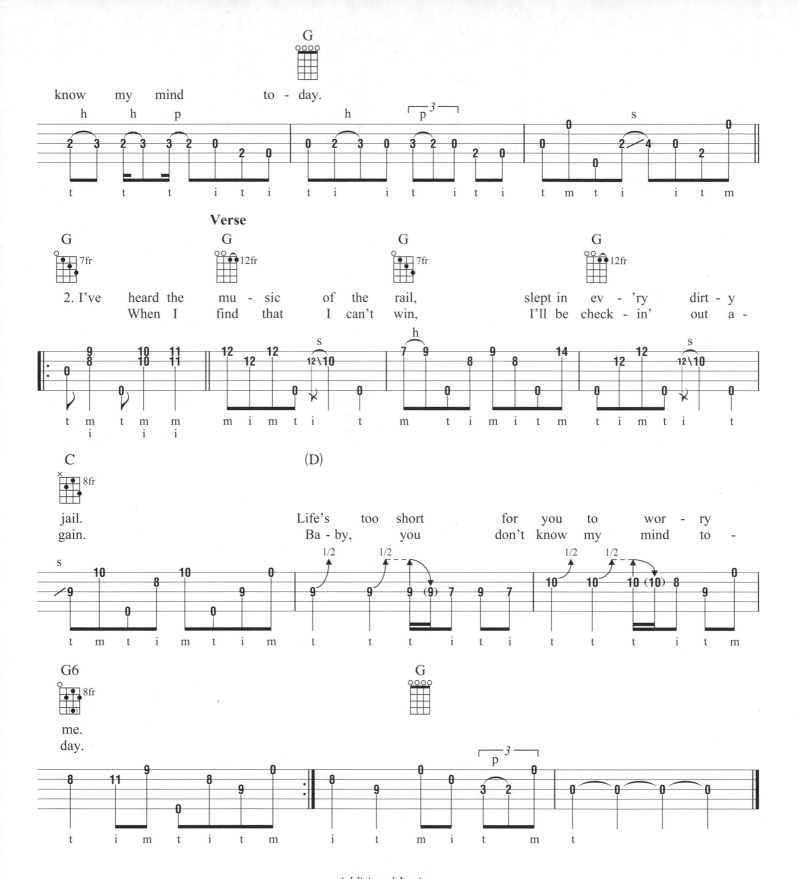

Additional Lyrics

3. I've been a hobo and a tramp, my soul has done been stamped.
   Lord, things I know I learned the hard, hard way.
   I ain't here to judge or plead, but to give my poor heart ease.
   Baby, you don't know my mind today.

4. Honey, you don't know my mind. I'm lonesome all the time.
   Born to lose, a drifter, that's me.
   You say I'm sweet and kind, and I can love you a thousand times,
   But baby, you don't know my mind today.

ABOUT THE AUTHOR

Fred Sokolow is best known as the author of over a hundred and fifty instructional and transcription books and DVDs for guitar, banjo, Dobro, lap steel, mandolin, ukulele and autoharp. Fred has long been a well-known West Coast multi-string performer and recording artist, particularly on the acoustic music scene. The diverse musical genres covered in his books and DVDs, along with several bluegrass, jazz and rock CDs he has released, demonstrate his mastery of many musical styles. Whether he's playing Delta bottleneck blues, bluegrass or old-time banjo, '30s swing guitar, a Tin Pan Alley uke song or a screaming rock solo, he does it with authenticity and passion.

Fred's other banjo books include:

- *Fretboard Roadmaps • 5-String Banjo*, book/soundfiles, **Hal Leonard LLC**
- *Complete Bluegrass Banjo*, book/soundfiles, **Hal Leonard LLC**
- *Beatles for Banjo*, book, **Hal Leonard LLC**
- *101 Banjo Tips*, book/CD, **Hal Leonard LLC**
- *Bluegrass Banjo Breaks & Licks*, book/soundfiles, **Hal Leonard LLC**
- *Instant Banjo*, book/soundfiles, **Hal Leonard LLC**
- *Blues Banjo*, book/soundfiles, **Hal Leonard LLC**

Email Fred with any questions about this or his other banjo books at: **Sokolowmusic.com**.